KIDS

SP

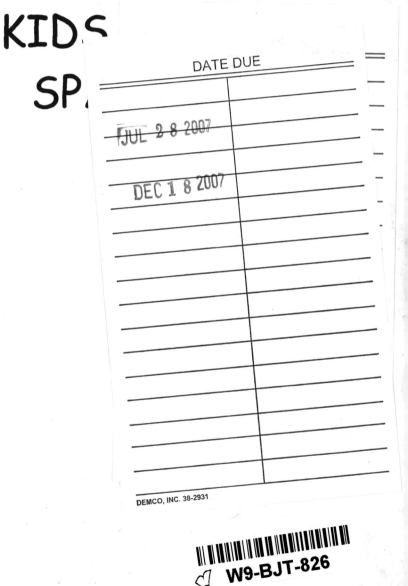
W9-BJT-826

KIDS STUFF ---
SPANISH

Easy Spanish Phrases to Teach Your Kids (and Yourself)

Therese Slevin Pirz

BILINGUAL KIDS SERIES

CHOU-CHOU PRESS
P.O. BOX 152
SHOREHAM, N.Y. 11786
www.bilingualkids.com

Printed in the United States of America

First Edition.
Library of Congress Catalog No. 99-94904

ISBN   0-9606140-2-8

Order direct from the publisher:

Chou-Chou Press
P.O. Box 152
Shoreham, N.Y. 11786
www.bilingualkids.com

This book is dedicated to my brother,
Dick,
who is in my thoughts everyday—
with admiration
and love.

CONTENTS

ACKNOWLEDGMENTS

PREFACE

VOCABULARY

Note: To avoid the constant use of "he or she," and in the interest of clarity, the author has elected to use masculine pronouns in those chapters which contain paragraph information.

Child's name:_____

Received this book from:_____

Occasion:_____Date:_____

First indication of child's understanding Spanish:_____

_____

Child's first Spanish word:_____

Child's favorite Spanish word:_____

Favorite Spanish books or stories:_____

_____

_____

Favorite Spanish songs:_____

Favorite Spanish musical group:_____

Favorite Spanish celebrities:_____

_____

Favorite things to do in Spanish:_____

_____

_____

Favorite Spanish foods:_____

_____

_____

ACKNOWLEDGMENTS

I wish to thank Tara Kelly of Rome, Italy for her support, expertise and electronic savvy. Besides her technical know-how, she is a source of limitless energy and enthusiasm.

I also wish to acknowledge the advice and interest extended by Marianne and Peter Hennessey.

Susanna Perez and Alfredo Ambrozevicius translated sentences and answered questions promptly and kindly in the midst of their busy schedules.

Above all I wish to acknowledge my "partner" and husband, Joe, who has helped me and worked with me on many more projects than this book.

PREFACE

This book covers the range of children's interests from infancy to teens. It is meant to cover not so much the calendar age of children but rather their activities and interests regardless of what birthdays they have passed. This perspective has been taken because children develop at different rates, and it is hard to predict where they will be and what their experiences will be at any particular age.

The author has researched many books in preparation for the *KIDS STUFF SERIES* and has found this series to be unique because it translates phrases and sentences which are child-based. Because of this perspective, the *KIDS STUFF SERIES* enables the user to speak *to* children, to carry on a conversation *with* children, and to model sentences that children can use in replying to others.

Whatever age you begin your foreign language adventure you will find this book an invaluable source for your journey. Good luck with this adventure. Make it FUN! (The longest chapters are "Fun," and "Saturday Afternoon"!)

Lo tengo en la punta de la lengua. It's on the tip of my tongue.

HOLA | GREETINGS

Start your day and your conversations here. Saying the first few words in Spanish will help you build momentum to continue the rest of the conversation, the rest of the activity, the rest of the day-- in Spanish. Spanish is such a lively language. Hearing it will make you feel cheerful especially when it is spoken by you or to you. ¡Hola!

¡Diga! ¡Digame!
¡DEE-gah! ¡DEE-gah-meh!

Hello! (Answering the phone)   *

¿Quién habla?
¿K'YEHN AH-blah?

Who's speaking?

Buenos días.
BWEH-nohs DEE-ahs.

Good morning. Hello.

Buenas tardes.
BWEH-nahs TAHR-dehs.

Good evening. (Before 9 p.m.)

¿Me extrañas?
¿Meh ehs-TRAHN-yahs?

Do you miss me?

¿Me extrañaste?
¿Meh ehs-trahn-YAH-steh?

Did you miss me?

Dame un /abrazo/ beso/.
DAH-meh oon /ah-BRAH-soh/ BEH-soh/.

Give me a /hug/ kiss/. *

¿Cómo estás? ¿Qué tal?
¿KOH-moh ehs-TAHS? ¿Keh tahl?

How are you?
What's going on?

Muy bien. Gracias.
Mwee b'YEHN. GRAH-see-ahs.

Very well. Thank you.

¡Qué gusto de verte!
¡Keh GOOS-toh deh BEHR-teh!

How nice to see you.

¿Cómo va? Así así.
¿KOH-moh bah? Ah-SEE ah-SEE.

How goes it? So-so.

Buenas noches.
BWEH-nahs NOH-chehs.

Good night. (After 9 p.m.)

Adiós. Hasta luego.
Ah-dee-OHS. AHS-tah loo-EH-goh.

Good-bye. See you later.

¿En qué puedo servirle?
¿Ehn keh PWEH-doh sehr-BEER-leh?

How may I help you?
(Polite)

Di, "Adiós," "Chao."
Dee, "Ah-dee-OHS," "Chow."

Say, "Good-bye," "Bye-bye."

Perdón.
Pehr-DOHN.

Excuse me.

Buena suerte.
B'WEH-nah s'WEHR-teh.

Good luck.

Dios te bendiga.
Dee-OHS teh behn-DEE-gah.

God bless you.

¡Buen viaje!
¡B'wehn b'YAH-heh!

Have a good trip!

Cuídate.
KWEE-dah-teh.

Take care of yourself.

¡Salud!	To your health! (A toast or
¡Sah-LOOD!	sneeze)
¡Salud, amor y pesetas!	Health, love and money!
¡Sah-LOOD, ah-MOHR ee peh-SEH-tahs!	(A toast and wish)
¡Feliz Cumpleaños!	Happy Birthday! *
¡Feh-LEES koom-pleh-AHN-yohs!	
¡Feliz Navidad!	Merry Christmas! *
¡Feh-LEES nah-bee-DAHD!	
¡Prospero Año Nuevo!	Happy New Year!
¡Prohs-PEH-roh AHN-yoh NWEH-boh!	
Por favor.	Please.
Pohr fah-BOHR.	
(No) gracias.	(No) thank you.
(Noh) GRAH-see-ahs.	
No hace falta.	You don't have to do that.
Noh AH-seh FAHL-tah.	
De nada.	You're welcome.
Deh NAH-dah.	
¡Bienvenidos!	Welcome!
¡B'yehn-behn-EE-dohs!	
Encantado/a. (m/f)	Pleased to meet you.
Ehn-kahn-TAH-doh/ dah.	
¿Cómo te llamas?	What is your name?
¿KOH-moh teh YAH-mahs?	
Me llamo...	My name is...
Meh YAH-moh...	
Pasa un buen día.	Have a nice day. *
PAH-sah oon b'wehn DEE-ah.	

De la cabeza a los pies... From head to toe...

LA SALA *de* BAÑO

BATHROOM

¿Tienes que ir al baño?
¿T'YEH-nehs keh eer ahl BAH-n'yoh?

Do you need to go to
the bathroom?

Dime cuando tienes que ir al baño.
DEE-meh KWAHN-doh t'YEH-nehs keh
eer ahl BAH-n'yoh.

Tell me when you have
to go to the bathroom.

Me dijiste que tienes que ir al baño.
Meh dee-HEES-teh keh t'YEH-nehs
keh eer ahl BAH-n'yoh.

You told me that you had
to go to the bathroom.

Tira de la cadena.
TEE-rah deh lah kah-DEH-nah.

Flush the toilet.

Baja la silla.
BAH-hah lah SEE-yah.

Put down the (toilet) seat.

Ve a lavarte. Dúchate.
Beh ah lah-BAHR-teh. DOO-chah-teh.

Go get washed. Take a
shower.

Tu cara está sucia. Lávala.
Too KAH-rah ehs-TAH SOO-s'yah.
LAH-bah-lah.

Your face is dirty. Wash it.

No te olvides de lavarte las manos.
Noh teh ohl-BEE-dehs deh lah-BAHR-teh
lahs MAH-nohs.

Don't forget to wash
your hands.

¿Te lavaste el cuello?
¿Teh lah-BAHS-teh el KWEH-yoh?

Did you wash your neck?

Límpiate las uñas.
LEEM-p'yah-teh lahs OON-yahs.

Clean your fingernails.

Lávate los dientes.
LAH-bah-teh lohs d'YEHN-tehs.

Brush your teeth.

Usa hilo dental.
OO-sah EE-loh dehn-TAHL.

Use floss.

Tu cepillo de dientes está en el lavamanos.
Too seh-PEE-yoh deh d'YEHN-tehs ehs-
TAH ehn el lah-bah-MAH-nohs.

Your toothbrush is on the ⋆
sink.

Limpia bien detrás de las orejas.
LEEM-p'yah b'YEHN deh-TRAHS deh
lahs oh-REH-hahs.

Scrub behind your ears.

No te lavaste la cara.
Noh teh lah-BAHS-teh lah KAH-rah.

You didn't wash your face.

Las manos y la cara están limpias.
Lahs MAH-nohs ee lah KAH-rah ehs-TAHN
LEEM-p'yahs.

Your hands and face are clean.

¡Bien! Ahora estás limpio/a/. (m/f)
¡B'YEHN! Ah-OH-rah ehs-TAHS
LEEM-p'yoh/ yah/.

Good! Now you look clean.

Necesitas tomar un baño.
Neh-seh-SEE-tahs toh-MAHR oon BAH-n'yoh.

You need to take a bath.

/Abre/ Cierra/ el grifo.
/AH-breh/ S'YEH-rrah/ el GREE-foh.

Turn /on/ off/ the water.

17

¿Estás tomando un baño?
¿Ehs-TAHS toh-MAHN-doh oon BAH-n'yoh?

Are you taking a bath?

Te estoy llenando el baño.
Teh ehs-TOY yeh-NAHN-doh el BAH-n'yoh.

I'm running a bath for you.

¿Ves correr el agua?
¿Behs koh-RREHR el AH-gwah?

See the water run?

El agua está/ demasiado caliente/
demasiado fría/ perfecta/.
El AH-gwah ehs-TAH/ deh-mah-s'YAH-doh
kah-l'YEHN-teh / deh-mah-s'YAH-doh
FREE-ah / pehr-FEHK-tah/.

The water is / too hot/ too
cold/ just right/.

No llenes la bañera con demasiada agua.
Noh YEH-nehs lah bah-n'YEH-rah kohn
deh-mah-s'YAH-dah AH-gwah.

Don't fill the tub with too
much water.   *

Estoy lavandote /el cuello/ la espalda/
las rodillas/.
Ehs-TOY lah-BAHN-doh-teh/ el KWEH-
yoh/ lah ehs-PAHL-dah/ lahs rroh-DEE-yahs/.

I'm washing / your neck/
your back/ your knees/.

Usa bastante jabón.
OO-sah bah-STAHN-teh hah-BOHN.

Use plenty of soap. *

El jabón huele bien, pero está resbaladizo.
El hah-BOHN oo-WHEH-leh b'YEHN, PEH-
roh ehs-TAH rrehs-bah-lah-DEE-soh.

The soap smells good, but
it is slippery.   *

No necesitas tanto:
  jabón (hah-BOHN),
  agua (AH-gwah),
  pasta de dientes (PAH-stah deh d'-EHN-tehs),
  desodorante (dehs-oh-dohr-AHN-teh),
  maquillaje (mah-kee-AH-heh).

You don't need so much:
  soap,
  water,
  toothpaste,
  deodorant,
  make-up.

Sécate bien.
SEH-kah-teh b'YEHN.

Dry yourself well.

18

/Vacía / Limpia/ la bañera.
/Bah-SEE-yah/ LEEM-p'yah /lah
bah-n'YEH-rah.

/Empty/ Clean/ the tub.

Dobla la toalla.
DOH-blah lah toh-IGH-yah.

Fold the towel. *

Pon la toalla en el lavado.
Pohn lah toh-IGH-yah ehn el lah-BAH-doh.

Put the towel in the laundry.

Cuelga la toallita de la cara.
K'WEHL-gah lah toh-igh-YEE-tah
deh lah KAH-rah.

Hang up the face cloth.

¿Apagaste la luz?
¿Ah-pah-GAHS-teh lah loos?

Did you turn off the light?

¿Te gusta el baño?
¿Teh GOOS-tah el BAH-n'yoh?

Do you like to take a bath?

Sí. Me gusta.
See. Meh GOOS-tah.

Yes. I like it.

¡La sala de baño es de toda la familia!
¡Lah SAH-lah deh BAH-nyoh ehs deh
TOH-dah lah fah-MEE-l'yah!

The bathroom belongs to
the whole family!

Creo que tú tienes que afeitar.
KREH-oh keh too t'YEH-nehs keh
ah-fay-TAHR.

I think you need to shave.

*

Lávate el pelo más tarde.
LAH-bah-teh el PEH-loh mahs TAHR-deh.

Wash your hair later.

Me sienta como un guante. It fits like a glove.

VESTIRSE

GETTING DRESSED

Is it to be the cowboy outfit or the space suit this morning? When you are in a hurry these are not options, I know. Perhaps, instead, when your little girl dresses her dolls or your little guy is playing with his action figures, you and they can try some of these phrases.

¿Dormiste bien?
¿Dohr-MEES-teh b'YEHN?

Did you sleep well?

¡Levantate! ¡Es hora de despertarte!
¡Leh-BAHN-tah-teh! ¡Ehs OH-rah deh
dehs-pehr-TAHR-teh!

Get up! It's time to wake up!

Estoy cambiandote el pañal.
Ehs-TOY kahm-b'YAHN-doh-teh
el pahn-YAHL.

I'm changing your diaper.

Mete la mano en la manga.
MEH-teh lah MAH-noh ehn lah MAHN-gah.

Put your hand in the sleeve.

Mete el pie en los pantalones.
MEH-teh el p'YEH ehn lohs pahn-tah-LOH-nehs.

Put your foot into your pants. *

Meto el pie derecho en el zapato derecho.
MEH-toh el p'YEH deh-REH-choh ehn el
sah-PAH-toh deh-REH-choh.

I am putting your right foot
into your right shoe. *

Metiste el pie en el zapato contrario.
Meh-TEES-teh el p'YEH ehn el sah-PAH-
toh kohn-TRAH-ree-oh.

You put your foot into the
wrong shoe.

Saca el brazo de la manga.
SAH-kah el BRAH-soh deh lah MAHN-gah.

Take your arm out of the
sleeve.

Yo te pongo las pijamas.
Yoh teh POHN-goh lahs pee-HAH-mahs.

I'm putting on your
pajamas.

Busca tus zapatos.
BOOS-kah toos sah-PAH-tohs.

Go get your shoes.

Me falta un zapato.
Meh FAHL-tah oon sah-PAH-toh.

I'm missing a shoe.

Abotona tu camisa.
Ah-boh-TOH-nah too kah-MEE-sah.

Button your shirt. *

¿Quieres llevar la blusa azul o la roja?
¿K'YEH-rehs yeh-BAHR lah BLOO-sah
ah-SOOL oh lah RROH-hah?

Do you want to wear the blue
blouse or the red one?

¿Dónde está tu sombrero?
¿DOHN-deh ehs-TAH too sohm-BREH-roh?

Where is your hat?

Cierra la cremallera de tu chaqueta.
S'YEH-rrah lah kreh-mah-YEH-rah
deh too chah-KEH-tah.

Close the zipper of your *
jacket. *

Busca tus guantes.
BOOS-kah toos GWAHN-tehs.

Look for your gloves. *

Papá se fue al trabajo.
Pah-PAH seh fweh ahl trah-BAH-hoh.

Daddy has gone to work.

Vístete.
BEES-teh-teh.

Get dressed.

Tenemos que vestirnos.
Teh-NEH-mohs keh beh-STEER-nohs.

We must get dressed.

No te muerdas las uñas.
Noh teh MWEHR-dahs lahs OON-yahs.

Don't bite your nails.

Ponte la ropa interior y los pantalones.
POHN-teh lah RROH-pah een-teh-r'OHR
ee lohs pahn-tah-LOH-nehs.

Put on your underwear and
your pants.

Lleva tu abrigo nuevo.
YEH-bah too ah-BREE-goh NWEH-boh.

Put on (Wear) your new coat.

Déjame ayudarte a amarrar el cordón
del zapato.
DEH-hah-meh ah-yoo-DAHR-teh ah ah-mah-
RRAHR el kohr-DOHN dehl sah-PAH-toh.

Let me help you tie your
shoe lace.
                                        *

Hay un nudo en el cordón del zapato.
Igh oon NOO-doh ehn el kohr-DOHN
dehl sah-PAH-toh.

There is a knot in your shoe
lace.

Péinate.
PAY-ee-nah-teh.

Comb your hair.

Cepilla tu pelo.
Seh-PEE-yah tu PEH-loh.

Brush your hair.

El cepillo, el peine y la lima están en
la cómoda.
El seh-PEE-yoh, el PAY-neh ee lah LEE-
mah ehs-TAHN ehn lah KOH-moh-dah.

The brush, comb and nail file
are on the dresser.
                                        *

La camiseta está bien.
Lah kah-mee-SEH-tah ehs-TAH b'YEHN.

The T-shirt will be fine.

A quien madruga, Dios le ayuda. The early bird catches the worm.

HORA *de* COMER

MEALTIME

¡Comamos!
¡Koh-MAH-mohs!

Let's eat!

¿Quieres el desayuno?
¿K'YEH-rehs el deh-sah-YOO-noh?

Do you want breakfast?

Ven y come tu cereal.
Behn ee KOH-meh too seh-reh-AHL.

Come and get your cereal.

¿A que hora almorzamos?
¿Ah keh OH-rah ahl-mohr-SAH-mohs?

When are we having lunch?

Tengo/ hambre/ sed/.
TEHN-goh/ AHM-breh/ sehd/.

I'm / hungry/ thirsty/.

¿Qué quieres comer?
¿Keh k'YEH-rehs koh-MEHR?

What do you want to eat?

¿Te sirvo más?
¿Teh SEER-boh mahs?

Would you like some more?

¿Algo más?
¿AHL-goh mahs?

Something else?

No has comido /nada/ en todo el día.
Noh ahs koh-MEE-doh /NAH-dah/
ehn TOH-doh el DEE-ah.

You have not eaten /anything/
all day.

La cena está lista. Siéntate.
Lah SEH-nah ehs-TAH LEES-tah.
S'YEHN-tah-teh.

Dinner is ready. Sit down.

Siéntate cerca de la mesa.
S'YEHN-tah-teh SEHR-kah deh lah MEH-sah.

Sit close to the table.

No pongas los codos en la mesa.
Noh POHN-gahs lohs KOH-dohs ehn lah
MEH-sah.

Don't put your elbows on
the table.

No te debas hablar con la boca llena.
Noh teh DEH-bahs ah-BLAHR kohn lah
BOH-kah YEH-nah.

You shouldn't talk with
your mouth full.

¿Quieres una merienda rica?
¿K'YEH-rehs OO-nah meh-r'YEHN-dah
RREE-kah?

Would you like a nice
snack?

¿Quieres tocino o papas?
¿K'YEH-rehs toh-SEE-noh oh PAH-pahs?

Do you want bacon or potatoes?

Sírvete.
SEER-beh-teh.

Help yourself.

Hazte un sándwich.
AHS-teh oon SAHND-weech.

Fix yourself a sandwich. *

¿Puedo tener más zanahorias?
¿PWEH-doh teh-NEHR mahs
sah-nah-oh-REE-ahs?

May I have more carrots?

¿Quieres más?
¿K'YEH-rehs mahs?

Do you want more?

¿Querrías más?
¿K'yeh-RREE-ahs mahs?

Would you like more?
(more polite)

¿Queda más para mí?
¿KEH-dah mahs PAH-rah mee?

Is there any more left for me?

Tomaré un poco más cereal.
Toh-mah-REH oon POH-koh mahs seh-reh-AHL.

I'll take a little more cereal.

No quiero más.
Noh k'YEH-roh mahs.

I don't want any more.

Ya tengo bastante.
Yah TEHN-goh bahs-TAHN-teh.

I already have enough.

¿Me dejas probar (tu helado)?
¿Meh deh-HAHS proh-BAHR
(too heh-LAH-doh)?

May I taste (your ice cream)?

No puedo comer más.
Noh PWEH-doh koh-MEHR mahs.

I cannot eat any more.

No tengo más de esto.
Noh TEHN-goh mahs deh EHS-toh.

This is all I have.

Pásame la sal, por favor.
PAH-sah-meh lah sahl, pohr fah-BOHR.

Pass the salt, please. *

Usa tu tenedor, cuchillo, cucharita.
OO-sah too teh-neh-DOHR,
koo-CHEE-yoh, koo-chah-REE-tah.

Use your fork, knife, spoon.

No aprietes el plátano en tu mano.
Noh ah-pree-EH-tehs el PLAH-tah-noh
ehn too MAH-noh.

Don't squeeze the banana in
your hand.   *

Come la manzana madura, pero ten cuidado
con las semillas.   .
KOH-meh lah mahn-SAH-nah mah-DOO-rah,
PEH-roh tehn kwee-DAH-doh kohn lahs
seh-MEE-yahs.

Eat the ripe apple, but be careful of the pits.   *

25

Déjame cortar la carne.
DEH-hah-meh kohr-TAHR lah KAHR-neh.

Let me cut your meat.

¿Alguien quiere perritos calientes?
¿AHL-gee-ehn k'YEH-reh peh-RREE-tohs
kah-l'YEHN-tehs?

Would anyone like hot dogs? *

No tomes la leche con tanta prisa.
Noh TOH-mehs lah LEH-cheh kohn
TAHN-tah PREE-sah.

Don't drink your milk so fast.

Come un poco solamente.
KOH-meh oon POH-koh soh-lah-MEHN-teh.

Eat just a little.

Qué aroma tan bueno.
Keh ah-ROH-mah tahn BWEH-noh.

The food smells good.

Es agrio/ a/. (m/f)
Ehs ah-GREE-oh/ah/.

It is sour.

El café es amargo.
El kah-FEH ehs ah-MAHR-goh.

The coffee is bitter.

El postre es dulce.
El POHS-treh ehs DOOL-seh.

The dessert is sweet. *

La salsa es muy blanda.
Lah SAHL-sah ehs mwee BLAHN-dah.

The sauce is bland.

El pescado está demasiado salado.
El pehs-KAH-doh ehs-TAH deh-mah-
s'YAH-doh sah-LAH-doh.

The fish is too salty. *

El biftec es jugoso.
El beef-TEHK ehs hoo-GOH-soh.

The steak is juicy.

¿Te gusta el queso?
¿Teh GOOS-tah el KEH-soh?

Do you like cheese?

¿Te gustaría un sorbito de té?
¿Teh goos-tah-REE-ah oon sohr-BEE-toh
deh teh?

Would you like a sip of tea?

26

Come tu espinaca.
KOH-meh too ehs-pee-NAH-kah.

Eat your spinach.

Me gustan las judías verdes.
Meh GOOS-tahn lahs hoo-DEE-ahs
BEHR-dehs.

I like stringbeans. *

Puedes darte de comer solo/a.
Inténtalo.
PWEH-dehs DAHR-teh deh koh-MEHR
SOH-loh /lah. Een-TEHN-tah-loh.

You can feed yourself.
Try it.

Tienes comida en toda la cara.
T'YEHN-ehs koh-MEE-dah ehn TOH-dah
lah KAH-rah.

You have food all over
your face.

No hables con la boca llena.
Noh AH-blehs kohn lah BOH-kah YEH-nah.

Don't speak with your
mouth full.

Sirve la leche en el vaso.
SEER-beh lah LEH-cheh ehn el BAH-soh.

Pour the milk in the glass.

Alguien dejó un poco de leche en el vaso.
AHL-gee-ehn deh-HOH oon POH-koh deh
LEH-cheh ehn el BAH-soh.

Someone left some milk
in the glass.

Corta el pan con cuidado.
KOHR-tah el pahn kohn kwee-DAH-doh.

Cut the bread carefully. *

No llenes el vaso.
Noh YEH-nehs el BAH-soh.

Don't fill the glass.

No desparrames el agua.
Noh dehs-pah-RRAH-mehs el AH-gwah.

Don't spill the water.

¿Por qué tienes que comer tanto?
¿Pohr KEH t'YEHN-ehs keh koh-MEHR
TAHN-toh?

Why must you eat so
much?

Toma todo el jugo.
TOH-mah TOH-doh el HOO-goh.

Finish your juice.

27

¿Podrás darme un bocado?
¿Poh-DRAHS DAHR-meh oon boh-KAH-doh?

Will you give me a bite?

¿Has terminado de comer?
¿Ahs tehr-mee-NAH-doh deh koh-MEHR?

Have you finished eating?

Eso es todo.
EH-soh ehs TOH-doh.

All gone.

Comiste todo lo que estaba en el plato.
Koh-MEES-teh TOH-doh loh keh
ehs-TAH-bah ehn el PLAH-toh.

You have eaten everything
on your plate.

¡Buen provecho!
¡Bwehn proh-BEH-choh!

Enjoy your meal!

¡Ay! ¡Qué rico/a! (m/f)
¡Igh! ¡Keh RREE-koh/kah!

Oh! How delicious!

¡Qué buena cena!
¡Keh b'WEH-nah SEH-nah!

What a good meal!

28

Quien bien te quiere te hará llorar. Spare the rod and spoil the child.

INSTRUCCIONES	DIRECTIONS

These are the pages you use to enlist, explain, persuade, coax, and insist with your child. When all else fails, there's always, "...porque yo lo dije." ("...because I said so.") --- appropriate justification in any language.

¿Qué es /eso/ esto/?	What is/ that/this/?
¿Keh ehs /EH-soh/ EH-stoh/?	
Es un caballo.	It's a horse.
Ehs oon kah-BAH-yoh.	
¿Qué oyes?	What do you hear?
¿Keh OY-ehs?	
¡Qué ruido (espantoso)!	What a (terrible) noise!
¡Keh rr'WEE-doh (ehs-pahn-TOH-soh)!	
¿Te he asustado?	Did I frighten you?
¿Teh eh ah-soos-TAH-doh?	
¡Vamos!	Come on!
¡BAH-mohs!	
¿Qué dices?	What are you saying?
¿Keh DEE-sehs?	

¿Qué dijiste?
¿Keh dee-HEE-steh?

What did you say?

Yo (te) escucho.
Yoh (teh) ehs-KOO-choh.

I'm listening (to you).

¡Qué bien cantas!
¡Keh b'YEHN KAHN-tahs!

How well you sing!

¡Qué hablador/a/ eres! (m/f)
¡Keh ah-blah-DOHR/ ah/ EH-rehs!

How talkative you are!

¡Siéntate (recto/ a)! (m/f)
¡S'YEHN-tah-teh (RREHK-toh/tah)!

Sit up (straight)!

Siéntate en mi regazo.
S'YEHN-tah-teh ehn mee rreh-GAH-soh.

Sit on my lap.

Levanta la cabeza.
Leh-BAHN-tah lah kah-BEH-sah.

Raise your head.

¡Mira, como fuerte!
¡MEE-rah, KOH-moh f'WEHR-teh!

Look, how strong!

¡Ten!
¡Tehn!

Hold it!

¡Ten el sonajero!
¡Tehn el soh-nah-HEH-roh!

Hold the rattle! *

¡Deja!
¡DEH-hah!

Let go!

¿Qué miras?
¿Keh MEE-rahs?

What are you looking at?

¿Qué piensas?
¿Keh p'YEHN-sahs?

What are you thinking about?

Yo veo que tú sueñas.
Yoh BEH-oh keh too SWEH-n'yahs.

I can see that you are dreaming.

Mueve los brazos y las piernas.
M'WEH-beh lohs BRAH-sohs ee
lahs p'YEHR-nahs.

Move your arms and legs.

¿Quién soy?
¿K'YEHN soy?

Who am I?

¿Quién es?
¿K'YEHN ehs?

Who is it?

Yo te conosco.
Yoh teh kohn-OHS-koh.

I know you.

Es tu/ hermano/ hermana/.
Ehs too/ ehr-MAH-noh/ ehr-MAH-nah/.

It's your /brother/
sister/.

El es pequeño.
El ehs peh-KEH-n'yoh.

He is small.

Ella es pequeña.
EH-yah ehs peh-KEH-n'yah.

She is small.

Es /grande/ pequeña/.(f)
Ehs /GRAHN-deh/ peh-KEH-n'yah/.

It is /large/small/. (f)

Es /grande/ pequeño/. (m)
Ehs /GRAHN-deh/ peh-KEH-n'yoh/.

It is /large/small/. (m)

Tú tienes ojos como papá.
Too t'YEH-nehs OH-hos KOH-moh
pah-PAH.

You have eyes like
Daddy's.

¡Sonrie!
¡Sohn-REE-eh!

Smile!

Muéstrame una sonrisa grande.
MWES-trah-meh OO-nah sohn-REE-sah
GRAHN-deh.

Show me a big smile.

Aquí está tu nariz, tu boca, tu oreja.
Ah-KEE ehs-TAH too nah-REES, too
BOH-kah, too oh-REH-hah.

Here is your nose, your
mouth, your ear.

31

Quiero sacar tu foto.
K'YEHR-oh sah-KAHR too FOH-toh.

I want to take your picture. *

¡Alégrate esa cara!
¡Ah-LEH-grah-teh EH-sah KAH-rah!

Put a smile on your face!

¡Qué cuento lindo!
¡Keh KWEHN-toh LEEN-doh!

What a pretty story!

¿Lo te gusta, verdad?
¿Loh teh GOO-stah, behr-DAHD?

You like that, don't you?

Déjame darte masaje el estómago.
DEH-hah-meh DAHR-teh mah-SAH-heh
el ehs-TOH-mah-goh.

Let me massage your tummy.

¿Adónde vas?
¿Ah-DOHN-deh bahs?

Where are you going?

¡Date prisa!
¡DAH-teh PREE-sah!

Be quick!

¡No tan rápido!
¡Noh tahn RRAH-pee-doh!

Not so fast!

Levántate.
Leh-BAHN-tah-teh.

Get up.

Estate de pie.
Ehs-TAH-teh deh p'YEH.

Stand on your feet.

Date vuelta.
DAH-teh BWEHL-tah.

Roll over.

¿Ves...?
¿Behs...?

Do you see...?

¿Puedes tener el ratón?
¿PWEH-dehs teh-NEHR el rrah-TOHN?

Can you hold the mouse? *

¿Qué tienes en la /boca/ mano/?
¿Keh t'YEH-nehs ehn lah /BOH-kah/MAH-noh/?

What do you have in your /mouth/ hand/?

32

No pongas eso en la boca.
Noh POHN-gahs EH-soh ehn lah BOH-kah.

Don't put that in your
mouth.   *

Dámelo.
DAH-meh-loh.

Give it to me.

¡No des patadas!
¡Noh dehs pah-TAH-dahs!

No kicking!

¡No hagas saltar el agua!
¡Noh AH-gahs sahl-TAHR el AH-gwah!

No splashing!

¡Como das patadas!
¡KOH-moh dahs pah-TAH-dahs!

How you kick!

¡Me estás mojando!
¡Meh ehs-TAHS moh-HAHN-doh!

You're getting me wet!

No llores. Está bien.
Noh YOH-rehs. Ehs-TAH b'YEHN.

Don't cry. It's O.K.

¿Por qué lloras?
¿Pohr KEH YOH-rahs?

Why are you crying?

¿Quién es ese en el espejo?
¿K'YEHN ehs EH-seh ehn el ehs-PEH-hoh?

Who's that in the mirror?   *

¿Quién te ama?
¿K'YEHN teh AH-mah?

Who loves you?

¿Te gustaría jugar a la pelota?
¿Teh goos-tah-REE-ah hoo-GAHR
ah lah peh-LOH-tah?

Do you want to play
with the ball?   *

Aquí está.
Ah-KEE ehs-TAH.

Here it is.

Vamos a visitar a abuelita.
BAH-mohs ah bees-ee-TAHR ah
ah-bwehl-EE-tah.

We're going to visit
Grandma.

Disponte a salir.
Dees-POHN-teh ah sah-LEER.

Get ready to go out.

Vamos a monstrarle como grande estás.
BAH-mohs ah moh-STRAHR-leh KOH-moh
GRAHN-deh ehs-TAHS.

We're going to show
her how big you are.

Quiero verlo/ la/.
K'YEH-roh BEHR-loh/ lah/.

I want to see/ him/ her/.

Ven a mami.
Behn ah MAH-mee.

Come to Mommy.

Vamos a ver como caminas.
BAH-mohs ah behr KOH-moh kah-MEE-nahs.

Let's see how you walk.

¡Mira esos dientes!
¡MEE-rah EH-sohs d'YEHN-tehs!

Look at those teeth!

¿Te duelen los dientes?
¿Teh DWEH-lehn lohs d'YEHN-tehs?

Do your teeth hurt?

¡No tan fuerte!
¡Noh tahn f 'WEHR-teh!

Not so loud!

¡No des voces!
¡Noh dehs BOH-sehs!

Don't shout!

¡Toca el tambor!
¡TOH-kah el tahm-BOHR!

Play the drum!

¡Toca la campanilla!
¡TOH-kah lah kahm-pah-NEE-yah!

Ring the bell! *

¡Qué linda música!
¡Keh LEEN-dah MOO-see-kah!

What beautiful music!

*

¡Toca otra canción!
¡TOH-kah OH-trah kahn-s'YOHN!

Play another song!

34

¡Aplaude!
¡Ah-PLOW-deh!

Clap!

Aquí hay un bebé como tú.
Ah-KEE igh oon beh-BEH KOH-moh too.

Here is a baby like you.

¿Dónde están los pies (del bebé)?
¿DOHN-deh ehs-TAHN lohs p'YEHS
(dehl beh-BEH)?

Where are the feet
(of the baby)?

Vamos a dar un paseo en tu coche.
BAH-mohs ah dahr oon pah-SEH-oh ehn
too KOH-cheh.

Let's take a stroll in
your carriage.

Tenemos que ir a la oficina del médico.
Teh-NEH-mohs keh eer ah lah oh-fee-SEE-nah
dehl MEH-dee-koh.

We have to go to the
doctor's office.

Es hora de reconocimiento.
Ehs OH-rah deh
rreh-koh-noh-see-m'YEHN-toh.

It's the time for a
check-up.

No tengas miedo.
Noh TEHN-gahs m'YEH-doh.

Don't be afraid.

Mami está aquí.
MAH-mee ehs-TAH ah-KEE.

Mommy is here.

Aquí vengo.
Ah-KEE BEHN-goh.

I'm coming.

¡Te voy a coger!
¡Teh boy ah koh-HEHR!

I'm going to get you!

¡Te cogí!
¡Teh koh-HEE!

Got-cha!

¿No te gusta...? (one item)
¿Noh teh GOOS-tah...?

Don't you like...?

¿No te gustan....?(more than one item)
¿Noh teh GOOS-tahn...?

Don't you like...?

35

Vamos a caminar un poco.
BAH-mohs ah kah-mee-NAHR oon POH-koh.

Let's take a little walk.

Toma mi mano.
TOH-mah mee MAH-noh.

Take my hand.

Siéntate en la silla.
S'YEHN-tah-teh ehn lah SEE-yah.

Sit in the chair. *

Quédate (allí) en el asiento.
KEH-dah-teh (ah-YEE) ehn el ah-s'YEHN-toh.

Stay (there) in your seat.

Cuidado con el escalón.
Kwee-DAH-doh kohn el ehs-kah-LOHN.

Watch the step.

Sube la escalera.
SOO-beh lah ehs-kah-LEH-rah.

Climb the stairs. *

Siéntate sobre el descansillo.
S'YEHN-tah-teh SOH-breh el
dehs-kahn-SEE-yoh.

Sit on the landing.

No te des vuelta.
Noh teh dehs b'WEHL-tah.

Don't turn around.

Baja la escalera.
BAH-hah lah ehs-kah-LEH-rah.

Come down the stairs.

¡Salta! ¡No Saltes!
¡SAHL-tah! ¡Noh SAHL-tehs!

Jump! Don't jump!

Dáselo (m) a papi.
DAH-seh-loh ah PAH-pee.

Give it (m) to daddy.

Dásela (f) a papi.
DAH-seh-lah ah PAH-pee.

Give it (f) to daddy.

Suéltalo.(m)
S'WEHL-tah-loh.

Let go of it.(m)

Dámelo. (m)
DAH-meh-loh.

Give it (m) to me.

36

No toques. No lo rompas.	Don't touch. Don't break it.
Noh TOH-kehs. Noh loh RROHM-pahs.	
Eso no va allí.	That doesn't go there.
EH-soh noh bah ah-YEE.	
Alcanza el cubo.	Reach for the block. *
Ahl-KAHN-sah el KOO-boh.	
Dale de comer a tu muñeca.	Feed your doll. *
DAH-leh deh koh-MEHR ah too	
moo-n'YEH-kah.	
Cuída bien a Tedi.	Take good care of Teddy.
KWEE-dah b'YEHN ah TEH-dee.	
	*
Dale té.	Give /her/him/ some tea.
DAH-leh teh.	
Hazle caricias al perro suavemente.	Pet the dog gently. *
AHS-leh kah-ree-SEE-ahs ahl PEH-rroh	
s'wah-beh-MEHN-teh.	
Deja de:	Stop:
DEH-hah deh:	
patear,	kicking,
pah-t'YAHR,	
pegar,	hitting,
peh-GAHR,	
morder,	biting,
mohr-DEHR,	
llorar.	crying.
yoh-RAHR.	
¡Basta!	Stop! Enough!
¡BAHS-tah!	

37

No:
Noh:

No:

patees,
pah-TEH-ehs,

kicking,

pegues,
PEH-guehs,

hitting,

muerdas,
m'WERH-dahs,

biting,

llores,
YOH-rehs,

crying,

comas.
KOH-mahs.

eating.

Eso (me) duele.
EH-soh (meh) d'WEH-leh.

That hurts (me).

¡No entres!
¡Noh EHN-trehs!

Don't go in. No admittance.

Dame la mano.
DAH-meh lah MAH-noh.

Give me your hand.

No me des...
Noh meh dehs...

Don't give me...

No hagas tanto ruido.
Noh AH-gahs TAHN-toh rr'WEE-doh.

Don't make so much noise.

Ven a decirlo a mi oído.
Behn ah deh-SEER-loh ah mee oh-EE-doh.

Come and whisper in my ear.

Soy todo oídos.
Soy TOH-doh oh-EE-dohs.

I'm all ears.

Silencio, por favor.
See-LEHN-s'yoh, pohr fah-BOHR.

Quiet, please.
(Gentle admonition)

Deja caer la voz.
DEH-hah k'YEHR lah bohs.

Lower your voice.

¡Callate!
¡KIGH-yah-teh!

Be quiet!
(Strong admonition)

No me preguntes otra vez.
Noh meh preh-GOON-tehs OH-trah behs.

Don't ask me again.

Estoy ocupado/ a /ahora. (m/f)
Ehs-TOY oh-koo-PAH-doh /dah/ ah-OH-rah.

I'm busy now.

Tengo prisa.
TEHN-goh PREE-sah.

I'm in a hurry.

Tengo que irme.
TEHN-goh keh EER-meh.

I must go

Tenemos que darnos prisa.
Teh-NEH-mohs keh DAHR-nohs PREE-sah.

We have to hurry.

Tenemos que irnos.
Teh-NEH-mohs keh EER-nohs

We must go.

Vuelvo más tarde.
B'WEHL-boh mahs TAHR-deh.

I'll come back later.

Vengo en un momento.
BEHN-goh ehn oon moh-MEHN-toh.

I'm coming in a moment.

¡Espera! (hasta que vuelva).
¡Ehs-PEH-rah! (AH-stah keh b'WEHL-bah).

Wait! (until I come back).

No te muevas.
Noh teh m'WEH-bahs.

Don't move.

No te vayas.
Noh teh BAH-yahs.

Don't go away.

¡Para!
¡PAH-rah!

Stop! (In place)

Deja de hacerlo.
DEH-hah deh ah-SEHR-loh.

Stop doing that.

Sal de allí.
Sahl deh ah'YEE.

Come away from there.

¡Haz lo que te digo!
¡Ahs loh keh teh DEE-goh!

Do as I tell you!

¡Y en sequida!
¡Ee ehn seh-GHEE-dah!

And right away!

Haz lo que quieras.
Ahs loh keh k'YEH-rahs.

Do what you like.

Platiquemos sobre este más tarde.
Plah-tee-KEH-mohs SOH-breh EHS-teh
mahs TAHR-deh.

Let's talk about this later.

¿Es de mi agrado?
¿Ehs deh mee ah-GRAH-doh?

Is it to my liking? Would I
like it?

No me des problemas.
Noh meh dehs proh-BLEH-mahs.

Don't give me trouble.

No me desobedezcas.
Noh meh deh-soh-beh-DEHS-kahs.

Don't disobey me.

¡Por turnos!
¡Pohr TOOR-nohs!

Take turns!

No se peleen.
Noh seh peh-LEH-ehn.

Don't quarrel with one
another. (more than one)

Déjalo/a quieto/a/.
DEH-hah-loh/ lah /kee-EH-toh/ tah/.

Leave /him/ her/ alone.

Deja el gato. No le molestes.
DEH-hah el GAH-toh. Noh leh moh-LEHS-tehs.

Leave the cat alone.   *
Don't tease him.

Deja eso.
DEH-hah EH-soh.

Leave that alone. Stop
that.

40

No toques eso. Está sucio.
Noh TOH-kehs EH-soh. Ehs-TAH SOO-s'yoh.

Don't touch that. It's dirty.

No tomes eso.
Noh TOH-mehs EH-soh.

Don't pick that up.

¡Saca las manos!
¡SAH-kah lahs MAH-nohs!

Hands off!

Abre la puerta.
AH-breh lah p'WEHR-tah.

Open the door. *

No cierres la puerta con llave.
Noh s'YEH-rrehs lah p'WEHR-tah
kohn YAH-beh.

Don't lock the door.

No abras la ventana.
Noh AH-brahs lah behn-TAH-nah.

Don't open the window.

No te apoyes por la ventana.
Noh teh ah-POH-yehs pohr lah
behn-TAH-nah.

Don't lean out the window.

Cierra la nevera.
S'YEH-rrah lah neh-BEH-rah.

Close the refrigerator.

No cierres la caja.
Noh s'YEH-rrehs lah KAH-hah.

Don't close the box.

Mueve la caja allí.
M'WEH-beh lah KAH-hah ah'YEE.

Move the box over there. *

¡Despacio!
¡Dehs-PAH-s'yoh!

Slow down!

¡No corras! ¡Camina!
¡Noh KOH-rrahs! ¡Kah-MEE-nah!

Don't run! Walk!

No te apures. Te vas a caer.
Noh teh ah-POO-rehs. Teh bahs ah
kah-YEHR.

Don't hurry. You're going to fall.

41

Toma tu tiempo.
TOH-mah too t'YEHM-poh.

Take your time.

Hazlo a tu paso.
AHS-loh ah too PAH-soh.

Take your time.

¡Apúrate!
¡Ah-POO-rah-teh!

Hurry!

No te quedas atrás.
Noh teh KEH-dahs ah-TRAHS.

Don't lag behind.

Come en la cocina para que no manches
la alfombra.
KOH-meh ehn lah koh-SEE-nah PAH-rah
keh noh MAHN-chehs lah ahl-FOHM-brah.

Eat in the kitchen so that
you don't stain the rug.

No te olvides de secarte los zapatos.
Noh teh ohl-BEE-dehs deh seh-KAHR-teh
lohs sah-PAH-tohs.

Don't forget to wipe your
shoes.

Pon el zapato en su lugar.
Pohn el sah-PAH-toh ehn soo loo-GAHR.

Put the shoe in its place.   *

El zapato debe estar en el suelo.
El sah-PAH-toh DEH-beh ehs-TAHR
ehn el s'WEHL-loh.

The shoe belongs on the floor.

Párate allí.
PAH-rah-teh ah'YEE.

Stand there.

No escribes en el muro.
Noh ehs-KREE-behs ehn el MOO-roh.

Don't write on the wall.

No toques la estufa.
Noh TOH-kehs lah ehs-TOO-fah.

Don't touch the stove.

Te vas a quemar.
Teh bahs ah keh-MAHR.

You're going to burn
yourself.

¿Te quemaste?
¿Teh keh-MAHS-teh?

Did you burn yourself?

42

No tengo nada.
Noh TEHN-goh NAH-dah.

There's nothing wrong
with me.

No juegues con fósforos.
Noh hoo-EH-guehs kohn FOHS-foh-rohs.

Don't play with matches. *

No vayas cerca de la escalera.
Noh BAH-yahs SEHR-kah deh lah
ehs-kah-LEH-rah.

Don't go near the stairs.

No cruze la calle.
Noh KROO-seh lah KAH-yeh.

Don't cross the street.

Mira los dos lados antes de cruzar.
MEE-rah lohs dohs LAH-dohs
AHN-tehs deh kroo-SAHR.

Look both ways before
crossing the street.

Espera la luz verde.
Ehs-PEH-rah lah loos BEHR-deh.

Wait for the green light. *

Desde ahora en adelante, ten cuidado.
DEHS-deh ah-OH-rah ehn ah-deh-LAHN-teh,
tehn kwee-DAH-doh.

From now on, be careful.

Ten/lo/ la/ por la manija/ con dos manos. (m/f)
TEHN/ loh/ lah/ pohr lah mah-NEE-hah/
kohn dohs MAH-nohs.

Hold it by the handle/
with both hands.

Presta atención a lo que haces.
PREH-stah ah-tehn-s'YOHN ah loh keh
AH-sehs.

Pay attention to what you
are doing.

No lo dejes caer en el suelo.
Noh loh DEH-hehs kah-YEHR ehn el
s'WEH-loh.

Don't drop it on the floor.

No te cortes el dedo; el cuchillo es agudo.
Noh teh KOHR-tehs el DEH-doh; el
koo-CHEE-oh ehs ah-GOO-doh.

Don't cut your finger; the
knife is sharp. *

No cojas eso.
Noh KOH-hahs EH-soh.

Don't grab that.

... porque yo lo dije.
... POHR-keh yoh loh DEE-heh.

...because I said so.

...porque es así.
...POHR-keh ehs ah-SEE.

... because that's the way it is.

¿Por favor, podrias...
(traerme la escoba)?
¿Pohr fah-BOHR, poh-DREE-ahs...
(trah-EHR-meh lah ehs-KOH-bah)?

Could you please...
(bring me the mop)?

¿Crees que... (podrias aydarme a hacer
el almuerzo) ?
¿KREH-yehs keh... (poh-DREE-ahs ah-yoo-
DAHR-meh ah ah-SEHR el ahl-m'WEHR-soh)?

Do you think that...(you
could help me prepare lunch)?

¿Crees que puedes...(llevar el plato)?
¿KREH-yehs keh p'WEH-dehs...
(yeh-BAHR el PLAH-toh) ?

Do you think you can...
(carry the dish) ?

¿Puedo preguntarte...(por qué tiraste
la piedra)?
¿P'WEH-doh preh-goon-TAHR-teh... (pohr
KEH tee-RAHS-teh lah p'YEH-drah)?

May I ask you...(why you
threw the rock)?

Vamos a tratar de hacerlo juntos.
BAH-mohs ah trah-TAHR deh ah-SEHR-loh
HOON-tohs.

Let's try to do it together.

Que /suba/ entre/ tu hermano.
Keh /SOO-bah/ EHN-treh/ too ehr-MAH-noh.

Have your brother /come
upstairs/ come in/.

Dile que venga.
DEE-leh keh BEHN-gah.

Tell him to come.

¡Entra!
¡EHN-trah!

Come in!

Golpea, por favor.
GOHL-peh-ah, pohr fah-BOHR.

Knock, please.

Ve a tu cuarto y ponte otra camisa.
Beh ah too k'WAHR-toh ee POHN-teh
OH-trah kah-MEE-sah.

Go into your room, and
put on another shirt.

Muestrame tu cuarto.
M'WEHS-trah-meh too k'WAHR-toh.

Show me your room.

¿Qué haces?
¿Keh AH-sehs?

What are you doing/
making?

Que lo haga/ el/ella/.
Keh loh AH-gah/el /EH-yah/.

Let /him/her/ do it.

Siéntate. Quédate sentado/a/.(m/f)
S'YEHN-tah-teh. KEH-dah-teh
sehn-TAH-doh/ dah/.

Sit down. Remain
seated.

Levántate. Quédate en pie.
Leh-BAHN-tah-teh. KEH-dah-teh ehn p'YEH.

Stand up. Remain
standing.

Acuéstate.
Ah-KWEHS-tah-teh.

Lie down.

Méce al bebé suavemente.
MEH-seh ahl beh-BEH s'wah-beh-MEHN-teh.

Rock the baby gently.

Dime lo que pasó.
DEE-meh loh keh pah-SOH.

Tell me what happened.

¿Fuiste tú quien hizo eso?
¿F'WEES-teh too k'YEHN EE-soh EH-soh?

Was it you who did it?

¿Lo hiciste a propósito?
¿Loh ee-SEES-teh ah proh-POH-see-toh?

Did you do it on purpose?

Cuidado con tu vocabulario.
K'wee-DAH-doh kohn too boh-kah-boo-
LAH-ree-oh.

Watch your language.

Quiero verlo/ la/.
K'YEH-roh BEHR-loh/ lah/.

I want to see/ him/ her/.

45

No eches votos!
Noh EH-ches BOH-tohs!

No cursing or swearing!

Quiero que me digas la verdad.
K'YEH-roh keh meh DEE-gahs lah behr-DAHD.

I want you to tell me the truth.

Habla más /lentamente/ claramente/.
AH-blah mahs /lehn-tah MEHN-teh/
klah-rah-MEHN-teh/.

Speak more /slowly/ clearly/.

No hables entre dientes.
Noh AH-blehs EHN-treh d'YEHN-tehs.

Don't mumble.

Escucha con cuidado.
Ehs-KOO-chah kohn k'wee-DAH-doh.

Listen carefully.

No te estás portando bien hoy.
Noh teh ehs-TAHS pohr-TAHN-doh
b'YEHN oy.

You are not behaving well today.

Prométeme que te vas a portar bien.
Proh-MEH-teh-meh keh teh bahs ah
pohr-TAHR b'YEHN.

Promise me to behave.

Pórtate bien.
POHR-tah-teh b'YEHN.

Behave yourself.

¿Entiendes lo que te digo?
¿Ehn-t'YEHN-dehs loh keh teh DEE-goh?

Do you understand what I'm saying?

No seas malo.
Noh SEH-ahs MAH-loh.

Don't be naughty.

¡Qué cabeza dura!
¡Keh kah-BEH-sah DOO-rah!

Are you stubborn!

No llores. Cálmate.
Noh YOH-rehs. KAHL-mah-teh.

Don't cry. Calm down.

No te pongas nervioso/ a/. (m/f)
Noh teh POHN-gahs nehr-bee-OH-soh/ sah/.

Don't be nervous.

46

No tengas miedo
Noh TEHN-gahs m'YEH-doh.

Don't be afraid.

Todo va a estar bien.
TOH-doh bah ah ehs-TAHR b'YEHN.

Everything is going to be all right.

¡Qué dolor!
¡Keh doh-LOHR!

That hurts!

Muéstrame donde te duele.
MWEHS-trah-meh DOHN-deh teh d'WEH-leh.

Show me where it hurts.

Tú tienes algunos rasgunos y moretones.
Too t'YEHN-ehs ahl-GOO-nohs rrahs-GOO-
nohs ee mohr-eh-TOHN-ehs.

You have some scratches and bruises.

Te gopeaste la nariz.
Teh goh-peh-AHS-teh lah nah-REES.

You bumped your nose.

Pásate la manita.
PAH-sah-teh lah mah-NEE-tah.

Rub it with your hand.

Abre la boca.
AH-breh lah BOH-kah.

Open your mouth.

No te pongas la piedrita en la boca.
Noh teh POHN-gahs lah p'yeh-DREE-tah
ehn lah BOH-kah.

Don't put the pebble in your mouth.

Siéntelo/ la/ con los dedos. (m/f)
S'YEHN-teh-loh/ lah/ kohn lohs DEH-dohs.

Feel it with your fingers.

No hagas caras.
Noh AH-gahs KAH-rahs.

Don't make faces.

No gimas.
Noh GIHM-ahs.

No whining, moaning.

Te hará bien.
Teh ah-RAH b'YEHN.

It will do you good.

Suénate la nariz.
S'WEH-nah-teh lah nah-REES.

Blow your nose.

Respira por la nariz.
Rrehs-PEE-rah pohr lah nah-REES.

Breathe through your nose.

No me digas eso.
Noh meh DEE-gahs EH-soh.

Don't tell me that.

Tienes una respuesta para todo.
T'YEH-nehs OO-nah rrehs-P'WEHS-tah
PAH-rah TOH-doh.

You have an answer for
everything.

Olvídate del juguete por un momento.
Ohl-BEE-dah-teh dehl hoo-GHEH-teh
pohr oon moh-MEHN-toh.

Forget your toy for a moment.

Usa tus propios juguetes.
OO-sah toos PROH-pee-ohs hoo-GHEH-tehs.

Use your own toys.

Acuérdate de llevar tus crayones.
Ah-k'WEHR-dah-teh deh yeh-BAHR toos
krah-YOHN-ehs.

Remember to bring your
crayons.   *

Tráeme...
TRAH-eh-meh...

Bring me...

Ven acá conmigo.
Behn ah-KAH kohn-MEE-goh.

Come here with me.

En seguida.
Ehn seh-GHEE-dah.

Immediately.

Ve al baño.
Beh ahl BAH-n'yoh.

Go to the bathroom.

Ve primero.
Beh pree-MEH-roh.

Go first.

Por acá. Sígueme.
Pohr ah-KAH. SEE-gheh-meh.

This way. Follow me.

¿(No) puedes hacerlo solo?
¿(Noh) p'WEH-dehs ah-SEHR-loh SOH-loh?

Can (Can't) you do it yourself?

Ve abajo y ayuda a abuelita.
Beh ah-BAH-hoh ee ah-YOO-dah ah
ah-bweh-LEE-tah.

Go downstairs and help
grandma.

Abuelo es corto de oído.
Ah-BWEH-loh ehs KOHR-toh deh oh-EE-doh.

Grandfather is hard of
hearing.

Ve/ afuera/ adentro/ a jugar.
Beh/ah-FWEH-rah/ ah-DEHN-troh/ ah
hoo-GAHR.

Go/ outside/ inside/ and
play.

¡Vamonos!
¡BAH-moh-nohs!

Come on! Let's go!

No apagues la luz.
Noh ah-PAH-ghehs lah loos.

Don't turn off the light.

Enciéndela otra vez.
Ehn-s'YEHN-deh-lah OH-trah behs.

Turn it on again.

No puedo ver en la oscuridad.
Noh PWEH-doh behr ehn lah
ohs-koo-ree-DAHD.

I can't see in the dark.

Empuja el botón.
Ehm-POO-hah el boh-TOHN.

Press the switch. ∗

Enciende el tocacintas.
Ehn-s'YEHN-deh el toh-kah-SEEN-tahs.

Turn on the cassette player.

Baja el aparato de discos compactos.
BAH-hah el ah-pah-RAH-toh deh
DEES-kohs kohm-PAHK-tohs.

Lower the compact disk
player.

Apaga la televisión.
Ah-PAH-gah lah teh-leh-bee-s'YOHN.

Turn off the television. ∗

49

No puedes mirar /este/ese/ programa.
Noh PWEH-dehs mee-RAHR/ EHS-teh/
EH-seh/ proh-GRAH-mah.

You may not watch
/this/ that/ program.

No televisión y tarea.
Noh teh-leh-bee-s'YOHN ee tah-REH-ah.

No TV when you are
doing homework.

Cuelga el teléfono.
K'WEHL-gah el teh-LEH-foh-noh.

Hang up the phone.

Deja de jugar juegos electrónicos /con la
computadora (nueva).
DEH-hah deh hoo-GAHR hoo-EH-gohs
eh-lehk-TROHN-ee-kohs /kohn lah
kohm-poo-tah-DOHR-ah (n'WEH-bah).

Stop playing computer games/
with the (new) computer.　*

Es demasiado tarde para tener amigos/gas/.
Ehs deh-mah-s'YAH-doh TAHR-deh
PAH-rah teh-NEHR ah-MEE-gohs/gahs/.

It's too late to have
friends over.

Eso (m) no es tuyo. (m)
EH-soh noh ehs TOO-yoh.

That one is not yours.

Esa (f) es tuya. (f)
EH-sah ehs TOO-yah.

That one is yours.

Este (m) es tuyo. (m)
EHS-teh ehs TOO-yoh.

This one is yours.

Esta (f) es tuya. (f)
EHS-tah ehs TOO-yah.

This one is yours.

Allí está/ el tuyo/ la tuya/. (m/f)
Ah'YEE ehs-TAH/ el TOO-yoh/ lah TOO-yah/.

There is yours.

El plazo de devolución de tu libro está vencido.
El PLAH-soh deh deh-boh-loo-s'YOHN deh too
LEE-broh ehs-TAH behn-SEE-doh.

Your book is overdue.　*

Devuelve el libro (a la biblioteca).
Deh-b'WEHL-beh el LEE-broh.

Return your book (to the
library).

50

Tienes/ práctica de fútbol/ lecciones de
música/ hoy.
T'YEHN-ehs/ PRAHK-tee-kah deh FOOT-
bohl/ leh-s'YOHN-ehs deh MOO-see-kah/ oy.

You have /soccer practice/
music lessons/ today.

Abrocha cinturón de seguridad.
Ah-BROH-chah seen-too-ROHN deh
seh-goo-ree-DAHD.

Fasten your seat belt.

¿Quién está entrampando la cuenta telefónica?
¿K'YEHN ehs-TAH en-trahm-PAHN-doh
lah KWEHN-tah teh-leh-FOHN-ee-kah?

Who's been running up
the phone bill?

Tienes que dar de comer al /perro/ gato/.
T'YEHN-ehs keh dahr deh koh-MEHR
ahl/ PEH-rroh/ GAH-toh/.

You have to feed the
/dog/ cat/.

Te toca a tí/ sacar el perro a pasear/ sacar
la basura/.
Teh TOH-kah ah tee/ sah-KAHR el PEH-rroh
ah pah-seh-AHR/ sah-KAHR lah bah-SOO-rah/.

It's your turn to / take the
dog for a walk/ take out the
garbage/.

¡Quítate los audífonos!
¡KEE-tah-teh lohs ow-DEE-foh-nohs!

Take off the head set! ∗

Sé en casa a la hora.
Seh ehn KAH-sah ah lah OH-rah.

Be home on time.

No llegues tarde.
Noh YEH-gehs TAHR-deh.

Don't be late.

¡No presentes quejas aquí!
¡Noh preh-SEHN-tehs KEH-hahs ah-KEE!

Complaints not accepted here!

Es hora de que te vayas.
Ehs OH-rah deh keh teh BAH-yahs.

It's time you were leaving.

Sé bueno. Sé buena.
Seh b'WEH-noh. Seh b'WEH-nah.

Be a good boy. Be a good girl.

51

No hay nada como el proprio hogar. There's no place like home.

AYUDANDO en CASA

HELPING at HOME

Your children are happiest when they are imitating adults in their lives. This includes the work they do. You and your children working together are a natural setting for speaking Spanish together.

Ayúdame a poner la mesa.
Ah-YOO-dah-meh ah poh-NEHR lah MEH-sah.

Help me set the table.

Puedes poner el mantel y las servilletas.
PWEH-dehs poh-NEHR el mahn-TEHL ee
lahs sehr-b'YEH-tahs.

You can put on the tablecloth and the napkins.

/Pon/Levanta/ la mesa, por favor.
/Pohn /Leh-BAHN-tah/ lah MEH-sah, pohr
fah-BOHR.

/Set/ Clear/ the table, please.

Ayúdame a / lavar/ secar/ los platos.
Ah-YOO-dah-meh ah/ lah-BAHR/
seh-KAHR/ lohs PLAH-tohs.

Help me / wash/ dry/ the dishes.

Ayúdame a / hacer la cama/ limpiar la casa/
lavar la ropa/.
Ah-YOO-dah-meh ah/ ah-SEHR lah KAH-mah/
leem-p'AHR lah KAH-sah/ lah-BAHR lah
RROH-pah/.

Help me/ make the bed/ clean the house/ do the wash/.

¿Hiciste la cama?
¿Ee-SEES-teh lah KAH-mah?

Did you make your bed?

¿Por qué no?
¿Pohr KEH noh?

Why not?

Tú haz de hacer tu cama.
Too ahs deh ah-SEHR too KAH-mah.

You're supposed to make your bed.

¡Me haces trabajar!
¡Meh AH-sehs trah-bah-HAHR!

You make me work!

Mami está barriendo el suelo.
MAH-mee ehs-TAH bah-rree-YEHN-doh
el s'WEH-loh.

Mommy is sweeping the floor.

Papi está pasando la aspiradora.
PAH-pee ehs-TAH pah-SAHN-doh lah
ah-spee-rah-DOHR-ah.

Daddy vacuums the rug. *

La aspiradora hace un ruido extraño.
Lah ah-spee-rah-DOHR-ah AH-seh oon
rr'WEE-doh ehs-TRAHN-yoh.

The vacuum makes a strange noise.

¡Qué polvo! Vamos a sacudir.
¡Keh POHL-boh! BAH-mohs ah sah-koo-DEER.

What dust! Let's dust.

Toma el paño en tu mano y frega. Así.
TOH-mah el PAHN-yoh ehn too MAH-noh
ee FREH-gah. Ah-SEE.

Take the dust cloth in your hand, and rub. Like this.

Estoy cosiendo una falda para la bebé.
Ehs-TOY koh-s'YEHN-doh OO-nah
FAHL-dah PAH-rah lah beh-BEH.

I'm sewing a skirt for the baby.

Ayúdale a tu padre a hacer la cena.
Ah-YOO-dah-leh ah too PAH-dreh ah
ah-SEHR lah SEH-nah.

Help father cook dinner.

Mamá está haciendo una torta.
Mah-MAH ehs-TAH ah-s'YEHN-doh
OO-nah TOHR-tah.

Mother is baking a cake. *

¿Me quieres ayudar a hacer galletitas?
¿Meh k'YEH-rehs ah-yoo-DAHR ah
ah-SEHR gah-yeh-TEE-tahs?

Do you want to help me
bake cookies?

Echa la harina.
EH-chah lah ah-REE-nah.

Pour in the flour.

Agrego el azúcar.
Ah-GREH-goh el ah-SOO-kahr.

I'll add the sugar.

Mezclo el azúcar y la mantequilla.
MEHS-kloh el ah-SOO-kahr ee lah
mahn-teh-KEE-yah.

I'm mixing the sugar and
the butter.   *

¿Necesitamos la levadura?
¿Neh-seh-see-TAH-mohs lah
leh-bah-DOO-rah?

Do we need baking powder?

Estoy revolviendo los huevos.
Ehs-TOY rreh-bohl-b'YEHN-doh lohs
WEH-bohs.

I'm beating the eggs.

Estira la masa.
Eh-STEE-rah lah MAH-sah.

Roll the dough.   *

Los cocemos en el horno.
Lohs koh-SEH-mohs ehn el OHR-noh.

We bake them in the oven.

Pon el reloj para media hora.
Pohn el rreh-LOH PAH-rah MEH-d'yah
OH-rah.

Set the clock for one-half hour.

Las galletitas están hechas.
Lahs gah-yeh-TEE-tahs ehs-TAHN EH-chahs.

The cookies are done.

No me puedes ayudar a planchar.
Noh meh PWEH-dehs ah-yoo-DAHR
ah plahn-CHAHR.

You cannot help me iron.

Me puedes ayudar a / separar/ doblar/ la ropa.
Meh PWEH-dehs ah-yoo-DAHR ah/ seh-pah-
RAHR/ doh-BLAHR/ lah RROH-pah.

You can help me/ sort/fold/
the laundry.

54

Después de limpiar, podemos leer un cuento.
Dehs-PWEHS deh leem-pee-AHR, poh-DEH-
mohs leh-EHR oon KWEHN-toh.

After cleaning, we can read a
story.

Antes de jugar, tienes que arreglar tu cuarto.
AHN-tehs deh hoo-GAHR, t'YEH-nehs keh
ah-rreh-GLAHR too KWAHR-toh.

Before playing, you must
straighten your room.

Repon todas las ollas en la alacena.
Rreh-POHN TOH-dahs lahs OH-yahs ehn
lah ah-lah-SEHN-ah.

Put all the pots back in
the cupboard.

¿Puedes ayudarme envolver el regalo?
¿PWEH-dehs ah-yoo-DAHR-meh ehn-bohl-
BEHR el rreh-GAH-loh?

Can you help me wrap the
present?

¡Qué maleza hay!
¡Keh mah-LEH-sah igh!

There are so many weeds!

Tenemos que quitar la maleza para que
crezcan las plantas.
Teh-NEH-mohs keh kee-TAHR lah
mah-LEH-sah PAH-rah keh KREHS-kahn
lahs PLAHN-tahs.

We need to weed the garden so
that the plants will grow.

Planta las semillas en una fila.
PLAHN-tah lahs seh-MEE-yahs ehn
OO-nah FEE-lah.

Plant the seeds in a row.

Ayúdame a cortar el pasto.
Ah-YOO-dah-meh ah kohr-TAHR el PAHS-toh.

Help me cut the lawn.

¿Me ayudarás a regar el jardín?
¿Meh ah-yoo-dah-RAHS ah rreh-GAHR
el hahr-DEEN?

Will you help me water the
garden?

No te esfuerces demasiado.
Noh teh ehs-FWERH-sehs deh-mah-s'YAH-doh.

Don't strain yourself.

No caves tanto.
Noh KAH-behs TAHN-toh.

Don't dig too much.

Cava un hueco pequeño aquí.
KAH-bah oon WEH-koh peh-
KEHN-yoh ah-KEE.

Dig a little hole here.

Ten cuidado de las orugas.
Tehn kwee-DAH-doh deh lahs oh-ROO-gahs.

Be careful of the caterpillars. *

¿Puedes rastrillar las hojas?
¿PWEH-dehs rrah-stree-YAHR lahs OH-hahs?

Can you rake the leaves?

Echa las hojas en el cesto de la basura.
EH-chah lahs OH-hahs ehn el SEHS-toh
deh lah bah-SOO-rah.

Throw the leaves into the
garbage pail.

No puedes podar los árboles.
Noh PWEH-dehs poh-DAHR lohs
AHR-boh-lehs.

You cannot prune the trees.

Es demasiado peligroso.
Ehs deh-mah-s'YAH-doh peh-lee-
GROH-soh.

It is too dangerous.

En vez de podar, puedes ayudarme a
hacer un carretón.
Ehn behs deh poh-DAHR, PWEH-dehs ah-
yoo-DAHR-meh ah ah-SEHR oon
kah-rreh-TOHN.

Instead of pruning you can
help me make a wagon.

¿Puedes lijar este pedazo de madera?
¿PWEH-dehs lee-HAHR EHS-teh peh-
DAH-soh deh mah-DEH-rah?

Can you sand this piece of
of wood?

Serrucha este tablero en dos partes.
Seh-RROO-chah EHS-teh tah-BLEH-roh
ehn dohs PAHR-tehs.

Saw this board in two. *

Dame el destornillador.
DAH-meh el dehs-tohr-nee-yah-DOHR.

Give me the screwdriver.

Martilla este clavo.
Mahr-TEE-ah EHS-teh KLAH-boh.

Hammer this nail. *

Tengo que trabajar en nuestro avión.
TEHN-goh keh trah-bah-HAHR ehn
n'WEHS-troh ah-bee-OHN.

I have to work on our
airplane.

¿Quieres mirar?
¿K'YEH-rehs mee-RAHR?

Do you want to watch?

Hay que pintar nuestro barco.
Igh keh peen-TAHR n'WEHS-troh BAHR-koh.

Our boat needs painting.

Tenemos que trabajar en el coche.
Teh-NEH-mohs keh tra-bah-HAHR ehn
el KOH-cheh.

We have to work on the car.

/Lava. /Aspira/ el coche.
/LAH-bah/ Ahs-PEE-rah/ el KOH-cheh.

Wash/ Vacuum/ the car.

Barre la acera.
BAH-rreh lah ah-SEHR-ah.

Sweep the sidewalk.

Necesitamos quitar la nieve.
Neh-seh-see-TAH-mohs kee-TAHR
lah nee-EH-beh.

We need to shovel the
snow.

Ayúdame conectar la computadora al monitor.
Ah-YOO-dah-meh koh-nekh-TAHR lah kohm-
poo-tah-DOHR-ah ahl MOHN-ee-tohr.

Help me connect the computer
to the monitor.

Aquí está la mesada.
Ah-KEE ehs-TAH lah meh-SAH-dah.

Here is your allowance.

57

Más alegre que unas pascuas. Happy as a lark.

CLASES *en* CASA   SCHOOL *at* HOME

A popular trend is taking place in America where many children and parents are taking charge of their own education. They are doing this at home. For those children who are having classes at home instead of in a school building these sentences will be useful. Of course, these sentences would apply to a classroom situation as well.

¡El autobús escolar acaba de pasar!   The school bus just went by!
¡El ow-toh-**BOOS** ehs-kohl-**AHR** ah-
KAH-bah deh pah-**SAHR**!

Es hora de empezar, tambien.   It's time for us to start, too.
Ehs **OH**-rah deh ehm-peh-**SAHR**,
tahm-b'**YEHN**.

¿Cuál es la fecha hoy?   What is today's date?
¿**Kwahl** ehs lah **FEH**-chah oy?

Hoy es el 14 de octubre.   Today is October 14.
Oy ehs el kah-**TOHR**-seh deh ohk-
TOO-breh.

¿Dónde quedamos ayer?
¿DOHN-deh keh-DAH-mohs ah-YEHR?

Where did we leave off
yesterday?

Necesitaremos cinta engomada, una
corchetera, tijeras, y papel de postes.
Neh-sehs-see-tah-REH-mohs SEEN-tah ehn-
goh-MAH-dah, OO-nah kohr-cheh-TEHR-ah,
tee-HEHR-ahs, ee pah-PEHL deh POHS-tehs.

We will need scotch tape,
a stapler, scissors, and
poster board. *

No hay /corchetes/ cola/.
Noh igh /kohr-CHEH-tehs/ KOH-lah/.

There are no /staples/
glue/.

Hay:
Igh:

There's:

    el proyecto de pescado,
    el proh-YEHK-toh deh pehs-KAH-doh,

      the fish project,

    el proyecto del barco,
    el proh-YEHK-toh dehl BAHR-koh,

      the boat project,

    el proyecto de mapa,
    el proh-YEHK-toh deh MAH-pah,

      the map project,

            a hacer.
            ah ah-SEHR.

        to do.

Necesito más tiempo para terminar el
proyecto.
Neh-seh-SEE-toh mahs t'YEHM-poh PAH-rah
tehr-mee-NAHR el proh-YEHK-toh.

I need more time to finish the
project.

¿Me ayudarías con la tarea?
¿Meh ah-yoo-dah-REE-ahs kohn lah tah-REH-ah?

Would you help me with
my homework?

No la entiendo.
Noh lah en-t'YEHN-doh.

I don't understand it.

No sé bien.
Noh seh b'YEHN.

I don't know for sure.

Chequee el tablero.
Cheh-KEH-eh el tah-BLEH-roh.

Check the bulletin board.

¿Para cuándo tengo que terminar el informe?
¿PAH-rah KWAHN-doh TEHN-goh keh
tehr-mee-NAHR el in-FOHR-meh?

By when do I have to finish
the report?

¿Tienes algo que hacer?
¿T'YEHN-ehs AHL-goh keh ah-SEHR?

Do you have something
to do?

En eso puedo aconsejarte.
Ehn EH-soh PWEH-doh ah-kohn-seh-HAHR-teh.

I can help you with that.

¿Tenemos que estudiar la ciencia?
¿Teh-NEH-mohs keh eh-stoo-d'YAHR
lah see-ehn-SEE-ah?

Do we have to study
science?

Me canso de /estudiar/ trabajar/.
Meh KAHN-soh deh /eh-stoo-d'YAHR/
trah-bah-HAHR/.

I'm getting tired of /studying/
working/.

Aquí está mi dibujo a la pluma.
Ah-KEE ehs-TAH mee dee-BOO-hoh ah
lah PLOO-mah.

Here are my pen and ink
drawings.

Lee para ti mientras que yo trabajo con
tu hermano.
LEH-eh PAH-rah tee m'YEHN-trahs keh
yoh trah-BAH-hoh kohn too ehr-MAH-noh.

Do your reading while I
work with your brother.

Sigue leyendo. Suma los números.
SEE-gay leh-YEHN-doh. SOO-mah
lohs NOO-meh-rohs.

Keep reading. Add the
numbers.

Con razón te gusta leer.
Kohn rah-SOHN teh GOO-stah leh-EHR.

No wonder you like to
read.

¿Quieres hacer la pregunta?
¿K'YEHR-ehs ah-SEHR lah preh-GOON-tah?

Do you want to ask a
question?

Muestra a tu hermana como hacer sus
problemas de matemática.
M'WEHS-trah ah too ehr-MAH-nah
KOH-moh ah-SEHR soos proh-BLEHM-ahs
deh mah-teh-MAH-tee-kah.

Show your sister how to do
her math problems.

Enseñate.
Ehn-SEHN-yah-teh.

Teach yourself.

Mami, el perforador está atascado.
MAH-mee, el pehr-foh-rah-DOHR
ehs-TAH ah-tahs-KAH-doh.

Mom, the hole punch is
stuck.

¿Podemos descansar un rato?
¿Poh-DEH-mohs dehs-kahn-SAHR oon
RRAH-toh?

Can we take a break for
a while?

Vamos a la cocina a buscar la merienda.
BAH-mohs ah lah koh-SEE-nah ah boos-
KAHR lah mehr-ee-EHN-dah.

Let's get a snack from the
kitchen.

Hagamos ejercicios físicos.
AH-gah-mohs eh-hehr-SEE-s'yohs FEE-see-kohs.

Let's exercise.

Trabajaremos en el jardín.
Trah-bah-hahr-EH-mohs ehn el hahr-DEEN.

We'll work in the garden. *

Cuando volvamos:
KWAHN-doh bohl-BAH-mohs:

When we come back:

leermos,
leh-EHR-mohs,

we'll read,

podemos conectarle al internet,
poh-DEH-mohs koh-nehk-TAHR-leh
ahl een-tehr-NEHT,

we can get on the Internet,

enviaremos correo electrónico,
ehn-bee-ah-REH-mohs koh-RREH-oh
eh-lehk-TROH–nee-koh,

we'll send e-mail,

hacermos galletitas para tío Pedro,
ah-SEHR-mohs gah-yeh-TEE-tahs PAH-rah
TEE-oh PEH-droh,

we'll bake cookies for Uncle
Peter,

pintaremos un dibujo para papi.
peen-tahr-EH-mohs oon dee-BOO-hoh
PAH-rah PAH-pee.

we'll paint a picture for daddy.

Fíjate en la pantalla.
FEE-hah-teh ehn lah pahn-TAH-yah.

Look at the screen (of the computer).

/El computador/ el teclado/ la impresora/ no funciona bien.
/El kohm-poo-tah-DOHR/ el teh-KLAH-doh/ lah eem-preh-SOH-rah/noh foon-s'YOHN-ah b'YEHN.

The /computer/ keyboard/ printer/ is not working well.

¿Cuándo se va a arreglar la computadora?
¿KWAHN-doh seh bah ah ah-rreh-GLAHR lah kohm-poo-tah-DOHR-ah?

When is the computer going to be fixed?   *

¿Habremos conectado mal los cables?
¿Ah-BREH-mohs koh-nehk-TAH-doh mahl lohs KAH-blehs?

Could we have connected the cables incorrectly?

Quiero/abrir/ cerrar/salvaguardar/ un archivo.
K'YEHR-oh /ah-BREER/ seh-RRAHR/ sahl-bah-gwahr-DAHR/ oon ahr-CHEE-boh.

I want to / open/ close/ save/ a file.

Las instrucciones que vinieron con la computadora están dificiles.
Lahs een-strook-s'YOHN-ehs keh been-ee-eh-ROHN kohn lah kohm-poo-tah-DOHR-ah ehs-TAHN dee-FEE-see-lehs.

The instructions that came with the computer are difficult.

No recuerdo mi palabra clave.
Noh rreh-KWEHR-doh mee pah-LAH-brah KLAH-beh.

I can't remember my password.

Me alegre que no tenemos que tomar exámen.
Meh ah-LEH-greh keh noh teh-NEH-mohs keh toh-MAHR ehk-SAH-mehn.

I'm glad we don't have to take an exam.

Tenemos que estudiar.
Teh-NEH-mohs keh ehs-too-d'YAHR.

We have to study.

A mí le faltan tres páginas para terminar de leer este libro.
Ah mee leh FAHL-tahn trehs PAH-hee-nahs PAH-rah tehr-mee-NAHR deh leh-EHR EHS-teh LEE-broh.

I have three pages left to reading this book.

Te dejo a tus tareas.
Teh DEH-hoh ah toos tah-REH-ahs.

I'll leave you to your work.

Necesito más tiempo para mi música.
Neh-sehs-SEE-toh mahs t'YEHM-poh
PAH-rah mee MOO-see-kah.

I need extra time for my music. *

¿Dónde está mi recorte?
¿DOHN-deh ehs-TAH mee rreh-KOHR-teh?

Where is my newspaper clipping?

¿Puedo omitir historia?
¿PWEH-doh oh-mee-TEER ees-TOHR-ee-ah?

Can I skip history?

Mis lápices de colores están perdidos.
Mees LAH-pee-sehs deh koh-LOHR-ehs
ehs-TAHN pehr-DEE-dohs.

My colored pencils are missing. *

¿Dónde estarán mis lápices?
¿DOHN-deh ehs-tah-RAHN mees LAH-pee-sehs?

Where could my pencils be?

¿Los habré dejado en el coche?
¿Lohs ah-BREH deh-HAH-doh ehn el KOH-cheh?

Could I have left them in the car?

¿Los ha visto alguien?
¿Lohs ah BEES-toh AHL-gee-ehn?

Has anyone seen them?

¿Quiero rayar con ellos.
¿K'YEH-roh rrah-YAHR kohn EH-yohs.

I want to draw lines with them.

¿Mami, dónde están los /limpiapipas/ limpiadientes/?
¿MAH-mee, DOHN-deh ehs-TAHN lohs/ leem-p'yah-PEE-pahs /leem-p'yah-d'YEHN-tehs/?

Mom, where are the /pipe cleaners/ toothpicks/?

¡Tú trabajaste mucho!
¡Too trah-bah-HAH-steh MOO-choh!

You did a lot of work!

Te mereces un premio.
Teh mehr-EH-sehs oon PREH-m'yoh.

You deserve a treat. *

Te quiero como las niñas de mis ojos. You're the apple of my eye.

ALABANZA   PRAISE

All the ways to say, "You're tops!" "None better!" " Wonderful, wonderful you!"
and many more expressions of encouragement. Use this chapter *often*. You and your
child will love it.

¡Qué linda voz!   What a beautiful voice!
¡Keh LEEN-dah bohs!

/Caminas/ dibujas/ hablas/ cantas/ bailas/ bien.   You/walk/ draw/ speak/ sing/
/Kah-MEE-nahs/ dee-BOO-hahs/ AH-blahs/   dance/ well.
/KAHN-tahs/ BIGH-lahs/ b'YEHN.

¡Qué bien /escribes/ nadas / juegas/!   How well you/ write/ swim/
¡Keh b'YEHN/ ehs-KREE-behs/ NAH-dahs/   play/!
HWEH-gahs/!

¡Eres maravilloso/ a/! (m/f)   You're wonderful!
¡EH-rehs mah-rah-bee-YOH-soh/ sah!

¡Eres brillante!   You're brilliant!
¡EH-rehs bree-YAHN-teh!

¡Qué dulce eres!   How sweet you are!
¡Keh DOOL-seh EH-rehs!

¡Qué / linda/ buen mozo / eres!
¡Keh /LEEN-dah/ bwehn MOH-soh/ EH-rehs!

How /pretty/ handsome/ you are!

¡Qué listo /a/ eres! (m/f)
¡Keh LEES-toh/ tah /EH-rehs!

How clever you are!

Qué mono/a/ eres. (m/f)
Keh MOH-noh/ nah/ EH-rehs.

How cute you are.

Este vestido te queda bien.
EHS-teh behs-TEE-doh teh KEH-dah b'YEHN.

This dress suits you well.

¡Qué ojos bonitos tienes!
¡Keh OH-hohs boh-NEE-tohs t'YEHN-ehs!

What pretty eyes you have!

Me encantan tus /ojos /manos/.
Meh en-KAHN-tahn toos /OH-hohs/MAH-nohs/.

I love / your eyes/ your hands/.

Me encanta tu pancita.
Meh en-KAHN-tah too pahn-SEE-tah.

I love your tummy.

¡Qué lindos rizos!
¡Keh LEEN-dohs RREE-sohs!

What pretty curls!

¡Qué buena chica!
¡Keh BWEH-nah CHEE-kah!

What a good girl! *

¡Qué buen chico!
¡Keh bwehn CHEE-koh!

What a good boy! *

¡Qué simpatico/a/ eres! (m/f)
¡Keh seem-PAH-tee-koh/ kah/ EH-rehs!

How nice you are!

Qué agradable.
Keh ah-grah-DAH-bleh.

That's nice of you.

Estás de buen humor.
Ehs-TAHS deh bwehn oo-MOHR.

You are in good spirits.

Me gustas. Te quiero.
Meh GOO-stahs. Teh k'YEH-roh.

I like you. I love you.

¡Bien hecho!
¡B'YEHN EH-choh!

Well done!

¡Diste en el blanco!
¡DEE-steh ehn el BLAHN-koh!

You hit the mark!

Es correcto.
Ehs koh-RREHK-toh.

That's correct.

Me gusta como juegas calladamente y
solito/ a. (m/f)
Meh GOO-stah KOH-moh hoo-EH-gahs
kah-yah-dah-MEHN-teh ee soh-LEE-toh/tah.

I like the way you play
quietly by yourself.

Fuiste muy amable en darme la toalla.
F'WEE-steh mwee ah-MAH-bleh ehn
DAHR-meh lah toh-IGH-yah.

You were nice to give me
the towel.

Sigue tratando. No te des por vencido.
SEE-gheh trah-TAHN-doh. Noh teh dehs
pohr behn-SEE-doh.

Keep trying. Don't give up.

¡Qué idea magnífica!
¡Keh ee-DEH-ah mahg-NEE-fee-kah!

What a magnificent idea!

Estás mejorando más y más.
Ehs-TAHS meh-hoh-RAHN-doh mahs ee mahs.

You're getting better and
better.

Ciertamente me ha gustado tu ayuda.
See-ehr-tah-MEHN-teh meh ah goo-STAH-
doh too ah-YOO-dah.

I certainly liked your help.

Limpiaste bien tu cuarto.
Leem-pee-AHS-teh b'YEHN too KWAHR-toh.

You cleaned your room well.

Fuiste paciente mientras hablaba por teléfono.
F'WEE-steh pah-see-YEHN-teh m'YEHN-trahs
ah-BLAH-bah pohr teh-LEH-foh-noh.

You were patient while I
was talking on the telephone. ✶

66

No todo lo que brilla es oro. All that glitters is not gold.

COMPRAS   SHOPPING

This is the area of foreign language conversation which may be unpredictable. When children are young, you can speak Spanish to them without restraint. However, as children grow more sensitive to other people they may not wish to appear "different" i.e., speaking a foreign language that others might overhear. Assure them that you understand their feelings. Resume speaking Spanish outside the store or in the car. Perhaps you might suggest that you and they "play store" at home using Spanish.

¿Quieres ir de compras?   Do you want to go shopping?
¿K'YEH-rehs eer deh KOHM-prahs?

Voy al mercado.   I am going to the market.
Boy ahl mehr-KAH-doh.

Necesito comprar...   I need to buy. . .
Nes-seh-SEE-toh kohm-PRAHR...

Tengo que devolver...   I need to return... (an item)
TEHN-goh keh deh-bohl-BEHR...

Hay una venta.   There's a sale.
Igh OO-nah BEHN-tah.

¡Qué gangas!   What bargains!
¡Keh GAHN-gahs!

67

¿Qué vas a comprar con tu dólar?
¿Keh bahs ah kohm-PRAHR kohn too
DOH-lahr?

What will you buy with your
dollar?

Vamos a tomar/el ascensor/la escalera
mecánica/.
BAH-mohs ah toh-MAHR/ el ah-sehn-SOHR/
lah ehs-kah-LEHR-ah meh-KAH-nee-kah/.

Let's take the /elevator/
escalator/.

Necesitas ropa nueva.
Neh-seh-SEE-tahs RROH-pah n'WEH-bah.

You need new clothes.

No podemos gastar demasiado dinero.
Noh poh-DEH-mohs gah-STAHR deh-mah-
s'YAH-doh dee-NEH-roh.

We cannot spend too much
money.

No podemos comprar eso.
Noh poh-DEH-mohs kohm-PRAHR EH-soh.

We cannot buy that.

Es demasiado caro/a/. (m/f)
Ehs deh-mah-s'YAH-doh KAH-roh/ rah/.

That's too expensive.

Quizás algo más barato.
Kee-SAHS AHL-goh mahs bah-RAH-toh.

Perhaps something cheaper.

Me falta dinero.
Meh FAHL-tah dee-NEH-roh.

I'm short of money.

/El vendedor/ la vendedora/ está allí.
/El behn-deh-DOHR/ lah behn-deh-DOH-
rah /ehs-TAH ah'YEE.

The salesclerk is over
there.

¿Cuánto cuesta?
¿KWAHN-toh KWEHS-tah?

How much does it cost?

¿/Lo/ la/ compramos? (m/f)
¿/Loh/ lah/ kohm-PRAH-mohs?

Should we buy it?

¿Qué número es este abrigo?
¿Keh NOO-meh-roh ehs EHS-teh ah-BREE-goh?

What size is this coat?

Déjame ver eso.	Let me see that.
DEH-hah-meh behr EH-soh.	
Pruébatelo/ la/. (m/f)	Try it on you.
Proo-EH-bah-teh-loh/ lah/.	
Te queda bien.	It looks good on you.
Teh KEH-dah b'YEHN.	
Yo me pongo en la cola (para pagar).	I'll get in line (to pay).
Yoh meh POHN-goh ehn lah KOH-lah	
(PAH-rah pah-GAHR).	
Cuenta el cambio.	Count your change.
KWEHN-tah el KAHM-bee-oh.	
¿Te gustaría ir conmigo:	Would you like to go with me:
¿Teh goo-stah-REE-ah eer kohn-MEE-goh:	
a la panadería,	to the bakery,
ah lah pah-nah-deh-REE-ah,	
al mercado,	to the grocery store,
ahl mehr-KAH-doh,	
a la lavandería,	to the laundromat,
ah lah lah-bahn-deh-REE-ah,	
al supermercado,	to the supermarket,
ahl soo-pehr-mehr-KAH-doh,	
al almacén,	to the department store,
ahl ahl-mah-SEHN,	
a la farmacia,	to the drug store,
ah lah fahr-MAH-see-ah,	
a la carnicería,	to the butcher shop,
ah lah kahr-nee-seh-REE-ah,	
a la juguetería,	to the toy store,
ah lah hoo-geh-teh-REE-ah,	

al banco, ahl BAHN-koh,	to the bank,
a la biblioteca, ah lah bee-blee-oh-TEH-kah,	to the library,
a la zapatería, ah lah sah-pah-teh-REE-ah,	to the shoe store,
al zapatero? ahl sah-pah-TEH-roh?	to the shoemaker?
Yo voy a aparcar. Yoh boy ah ah-pahr-KAHR.	I'm going to park the car.
No camines atrás. Noh kah-MEE-nehs ah-TRAHS.	Don't walk behind me.
¿Te gustaría ir conmigo: ¿Teh goo-stah-REE-ah eer kohn-MEE-goh:	Would you want to go with me:
al depósito de madera, ahl deh-POH-see-toh deh mah-DEH-rah,	to the lumber yard,
a la ferretería, ah lah feh-rreh-teh-REE-ah,	to the hardware store,
al semillero, ahl seh-mee-YEH-roh,	to the nursery,
a la estación de gasolina, ah lah eh-stah-s'YOHN deh gah-soh-LEE-nah,	to the gas station,
al aeropuerto, ahl ah-eh-roh-PWEHR-toh,	to the airport,
a la marina, ah lah mah-REE-nah,	to the marina,
al la tienda de animales? ah lah t'YEHN-dah deh ah-nee-MAH-lehs?	to the pet shop?

Es demasido:
Ehs deh-mah-s'YAH-doh:

This is too:

  apretado/ a/, (m/f)
  ah-preh-TAH-doh/dah/,

  tight,

  suelto/ a/, (m/f)
  SWEHL-toh/ tah/,

  loose,

  grande, (m/f)
  GRAHN-deh,

  large,

  pequeño/a/. (m/f)
  peh-KEH-nyoh/ nyah/.

  small.

Necesitamos comprar comida.
Neh-seh-see-TAH-mohs kohm-PRAHR
koh-MEE-dah.

We need to buy groceries.

Puedes sentarte en el carrito (del
supermercado).
PWEH-dehs sehn-TAHR-teh ehn el kah-RREE-
toh (dehl soo-pehr-mehr-KAH-doh).

You can sit in the
(shopping) cart.   *

Quédate en el carrito.
KEH-dah-teh ehn el kah-RREE-toh.

Stay in the (shopping) cart.

Mete los pies en las aberturas.
MEH-teh lohs p'YEHS ehn lahs ah-behr-
TOO-rahs.

Put your feet through
the openings.

No toques eso.
Noh TOH-kehs EH-soh.

Don't touch that.

¿Necesitas ir al baño?
¿Neh-seh-SEE-tahs eer ahl BAHN-yoh?

Do you need to go to
the bathroom?

Vamos a la sección de juguetes.
BAH-mohs ah lah sehk-see-OHN deh
hoo-GEH-tehs.

Let's go to the toy
department.

Cuantos más seamos mejor. The more the merrier.

¡DIVERSIÓN !   FUN !

If this chapter's pages don't have paint stains, water marks, tire tracks and gum sticking the pages together, you are not getting all there is to wring out of these pages! Be sure to write in some additional sentences and expressions you've learned elsewhere that are appropriate. I've found it helpful to jot sentences and phrases on 3 x 5 cards wherever I need them until the phrase is part of my thinking.

Tú puedes: You can:
Too PWEH-dehs:

jugar en el patio,   play in the yard,
hoo-GAHR ehn el PAH-t'yoh,

ir al patio de recreo,   go to the playground,
eer ahl PAH-t'yoh deh rreh-KREH-oh,

ir al campo (de fútbol, de béisbol),   go to the (soccer, baseball)
eer ahl KAHM-poh (deh FOOT-bohl,   field,
deh BAYS-bohl),

ir al /tu amigo/ tu amiga/.(m/f)   go to your friend's house.
eer ahl /too ah-MEE-goh/ too ah-MEE-gah/.

¿Te contentas con jugar en casa?	Are you satisfied with
¿Teh kohn-TEHN-tahs kohn	playing at home?
hoo-GAHR ehn KAH-sah?	

Pregúntales si quieren jugar:	Ask them if they want to play:
Preh-GOON-tah-lehs see k'YEH-rehn	
hoo-GAHR:	

al médico y enfermera,	doctor and nurse, *
ahl MEH-dee-koh ee ehn-fehr-MEH-rah,	

a la tienda,	store,
ah lah t'YEHN-dah,	

a mamá y papá,	mother and father,
ah mah-MAH ee pah-PAH,	

a la muñecas,	dolls,
ah lah moo-n'YEH-kahs,	

a rayuela,	hopscotch,
ah rrah-yoo-EH-lah,	

a vaqueros e indios,	cowboys and indians,
ah bah-KEH-rohs ee EEN-dee-ohs,	

a las escondidas,	hide and seek,
ah lahs ehs-kohn-DEE-dahs,	

a los juegos electrónicos.	computer games.
ah lohs hoo-EH-gohs eh-lehk-TROHN-	
ee-kohs.	

AIRPLANES (AVIONES)

Piloto a la torre de control.	Pilot to control tower.
Pee-LOH-toh ah lah TOH-rreh deh	
kohn-TROHL.	

Abróchense los cinturones.	Fasten your seat belts.
Ah-BROH-chehn-seh lohs seen-too-ROH-nehs.	

73

Estoy carreteando. Ehs-TOY kah-rreh-teh-AHN-doh.	I'm taxiing.
Estoy despegando. Ehs-TOY dehs-peh-GAHN-doh.	I'm taking off.
¿Podemos aterrizar? ¿Poh-DEH-mohs ah-teh-rree-SAHR?	May we land?
¡Se acabó la gasolina del avión! ¡Seh ah-kah-BOH lah gah-soh-LEE-nah dehl ah-bee-OHN!	We're out of gas!
¿En cuál vía podemos aterrizar? ¿Ehn kwahl BEE-ah poh-DEH-mohs ah-teh-rree-SAHR?	On which runway may we land?
Yo trabajé tres semanas haciendo mi avión. Yoh trah-bah-HEH trehs seh-MAH-nahs ah-s'YEHN-doh mee ah-b'YOHN.	I worked three weeks on my airplane.
¿Cuánto tiempo dura el vuelo a México? ¿KWAHN-toh t'YEHM-poh DOO-rah el BWEH-loh ah MEH-hee-koh?	How long does the flight to Mexico take? *

ANIMALS   (ANIMALES)

Mi trompa es larga; soy grande; y camino así. ¿Cuál animal soy? Mee TROHM-pah ehs LAHR-gah; soy GRAHN-deh; ee kah-MEE-noh ah-SEE. ¿Kwahl ah-nee-MAHL soy?	My trunk is long; I'm large; * and I walk like this. What animal am I?
Tengo dos jorobas; y me acuesto así. ¿Cuál animal soy? TEHN-goh dohs hoh-ROH-bahs; ee meh ah- KWEHS-toh ah-SEE. ¿Kwahl ah-nee-MAHL soy?	I have two humps; and I lie * down like this. What animal am I?

74

Ladro y gruño. ¿Cuál animal soy?
LAH-droh ee GROO-n'yoh. ¿Kwahl
ah-nee-MAHL soy?

I bark and growl. What
animal am I?   *

Pretendamos que somos canguros. Brinquemos.
Preh-tehn-DAH-mohs keh SOH-mohs kahn-
GOOR-ohs. Breen-KEH-mohs.

Let's pretend that we're
kangaroos. Let's hop.   *

Pretendamos que somos gallos. Vamos a
cacarear. ¡Qui-qui-ri-quí!
Preh-tehn-DAH-mohs keh SOH-mohs GAH-
yohs. Bah-mohs ah kah-kah-reh-AHR. ¡Kee-
kee-ree-KEE!

Let's pretend that we're roos-
ters. Let's crow. Cock-a-
doodle-do!   *

AUTOMOBILES   (AUTOMÓBILES)

El coche no se pone en marcha.
El KOH-cheh noh seh POH-neh ehn
MAHR-chah.

The car doesn't start. *

Se acabó la gasolina del coche.
Seh ah-kah-BOH lah gah-soh-LEE-nah dehl
KOH-cheh.

The car is out of gas.

No va más.
Noh bah mahs.

It doesn't go anymore.

¿Por qué no va el coche?
¿Pohr KEH noh bah el KOH-cheh?

Why doesn't the car go?

Empuja el coche.
Ehm-POO-hah el KOH-cheh.

Push the car.

Llénelo.
YEH-neh-loh.

Fill'er up.

Chequee el aceite, el agua y la batería.
Cheh-KEH-eh el ah-SEH-teh, el AH-gwah
ee lah bah-teh-REE-ah.

Check the oil, water and
battery.

75

¿Cuántos cilindros tiene?
¿KWAHN-tohs see-LEEN-drohs t'YEH-neh?

How many cylinders does it have?

Maneja el coche en el garage.
Mah-NEH-hah el KOH-cheh ehn el gah-RAH-heh.

Drive the car into the garage.

¡Date prisa!
¡DAH-teh PREE-sah!

Step on it!

Mi coche favorito es...
Mee KOH-cheh fah-boh-REE-toh ehs...

My favorite car is a.............

(BACKYARD)

(JARDÍN TRASERO)

Anda a jugar/ afuera /adentro/.
AHN-dah ah hoo-GAHR/ ah-FWEH-rah/ ah-DEHN-troh/.

Go/ outside/ inside/ to play.

Juega en/ el jardín/ la caja de arena/.
HWEH-gah ehn/ el hahr-DEEN/ lah KAH-hah deh ah-REH-nah/.

Play in/ the yard/ the sandbox/.

¿Quieres hacer burbujas?
¿K'YEH-rehs ah-SEHR boor-BOO-hahs?

Do you want to blow bubbles? *

No juegues en la tierra.
Noh HWEH-guehs ehn lah t'YEH-rrah.

Don't play in the dirt.

No recojas las flores.
Noh rreh-KOH-hahs lahs FLOH-rehs.

Don't pick the flowers.

Puedes nadar en la piscina si estoy contigo.
PWEH-dehs nah-DAHR ehn lah pee-SEE-nah see ehs-TOY kohn-TEE-goh.

You can swim in the pool if I am with you.

Salta del trampolín como te enseñé.
SAHL-tah dehl trahm-poh-LEEN KOH-moh teh ehn-seh-n'YEH.

Jump off the diving board as I showed you.

Ten cuidado cuando te encarames en los árboles.	Be careful when you climb trees.
Tehn kwee-DAH-doh KWAHN-doh teh ehn-kah-RAH-mehs ehn lohs AHR-boh-lehs.	
Los dos pueden sentarse en el carretón.	Both of you can sit in the wagon.
Lohs dohs PWEH-dehn sehn-TAHR-seh ehn el kah-rreh-TOHN.	
Hay lugar para dos.	There's room enough for two.
Igh loo-GAHR PAH-rah dohs.	
No salgas del patio.	Don't leave the yard.
Noh SAHL-gahs dehl PAH-tee-oh.	

BASEBALL   (BÉISBOL)

Te toca a tí.	It's you're turn.
Teh TOH-kah ah tee.	
/Coge/ tira/ la pelota.	/Catch/ throw/ the ball.
/KOH-heh/ TEE-rah/ lah peh-LOH-tah.	
Agarra el bate detrás de tí.	Hold the bat behind you.
Ah-GAH-rrah el BAH-teh deh-TRAHS deh tee.	
Mantén el ojo en la pelota.	Keep your eye on the ball.
Mahn-TEHN el OH-hoh ehn lah peh-LOH-tah.	
¡Batea! (el bate)	Swing! (the bat) *
¡Bah-TEH-ah! (el BAH-teh)	
¡Pega la pelota!	Hit the ball!
¡PEH-gah lah peh-LOH-tah!	
¡Perdiste! (la pelota)	You missed! (the ball)
¡Pehr-DEES-teh! (lah peh-LOH-tah)	(hitting or catching a ball)
Golpeas la pelota muy bien.	You hit the ball very well.
Gohl-PEH-ahs lah peh-LOH-tah mwee b'YEHN.	

BICYCLING   (CICLISMO)

Pon el pie en el pedal.
Pohn el p'YEH ehn el peh-DAHL.

Put your foot on the pedal.

¡No pedalea tan rápido!
¡Noh peh-dah-LEH-ah tahn RRAH-pee-doh!

Don't pedal so fast!

Trata de mantener el equilibrio.
TRAH-tah deh mahn-teh-NEHR el
eh-kee-lee-BREE-yoh.

Try to keep your balance.

Yo te estoy agarrando.
Yoh teh ehs-TOY ah-gah-RRAHN-doh.

I've got hold of you.

Déjame intentar.
DEH-hah-meh een-tehn-TAHR.

Let me try.

Agarra el manubrio.
Ah-GAH-rrah el mah-noo-BREE-oh.

Hold on to the handlebars.

Maneja/ todo derecho/ a la derecha/ a la
izquierda/.
Mah-NEH-hah/ TOH-doh deh-REH-choh/ ah
lah deh-REH-chah/ ah lah ees-K'YEHR-dah/.

Steer/ straight ahead/ straight/
left/.

Sigue pedaleando.
SEE-gay peh-dah-leh-AHN-doh.

Keep pedaling.

Andas muy bien en bicicleta.
AHN-dahs mwee b'YEHN ehn bee-see-
KLEH-tah.

You're riding your bicycle
very well.

Toca el timbre.
TOH-kah el TEEM-breh.

Ring the bell.

No andes en bicicleta en la calle. Hay
demasiado tráfico.
Noh AHN-dehs ehn bee-see-KLEH-tah ehn lah
KAH-yeh. Igh deh-mah-s'YAH-doh TRAH-
fee-koh.

Don't ride your bicycle in the
street. There's too much
traffic.

Vas demasiado rápido. Bahs deh-mah-s'-YAH-doh RRAH-pee-doh.	You're going too fast.
¡Frena! ¡FREH-nah!	Put on the brakes!
Tienes que ponerte el casco. T'YEH-nehs keh poh-NEHR-teh el KAHS-koh.	You need to put on your helmet.
¿Te lastimaste? ¿Teh lahs-tee-MAHS-teh?	Did you hurt yourself?

BOARD GAMES (JUEGOS de MESA)

¿Quieres jugar/ a las damas/ una partida de ajedrez/ juego de mesa/? ¿K'YEH-rehs hoo-GAHR/ ah lah DAH-mahs/ OO-nah pahr-TEE-dah deh ah-HEH-drehs/ hoo-EH-goh deh MEH-sah/?	Do you want to play/ checkers/ chess/ a board game/? ∗
¿Quién va? ¿K'YEHN bah?	Whose move it it?
¿A quién le toca? ¿Ah k'YEHN leh TOH-kah?	Whose turn is it?
Le toca a José. Leh TOH-kah ah hoh-SEH.	It's Joseph's turn.
Es /tu/ mi/ tourno. Ehs /too/mee/TOOR-noh.	It's / your/ my/ turn.
Tu pedazo está mal puesto. Too peh-DAH-soh ehs-TAH mahl PWEHS-toh.	Your piece is in the wrong place.
Yo tiro los dados ahora. Yoh tee-ROH lohs DAH-dohs ah-OH-rah.	I'll throw the dice now.
Yo quiero el azul. Yoh k'YEH-roh el ah-SUHL.	I want the blue figure. (piece) ∗

79

Eso no es jugar limpio. EH-soh noh ehs hoo-GAHR LEEM-pee-oh.	That's not playing fair.
Tienes que pagarme. T'YEHN-ehs keh pah-GAHR-meh.	You have to pay me.
Camina adelante. Kah-MEE-nah ah-deh-LAHN-teh.	Move forward.
Camina hacia atrás. Kah-MEE-nah ah-SEE-ah ah-TRAHS.	Move backward.
Estás ganando. Ganaste. Ehs-TAHS gah-NAHN-doh. Gah-NAHS-teh.	You are winning. You won.
Estás perdiendo. Perdiste. Ehs-TAHS pehr-dee-YEHN-doh. Pehr-DEE-steh.	You are losing. You lost.

BOATS   (BARCOS)

¡Abordo! ¡Ah-BOHR-doh!	All aboard! *
Nos hacemos a la vela para México. Nohs ah-SEH-mohs ah lah BEH-lah PAH-rah MEH-hee-koh.	We're sailing to Mexico.
¡El barco se está hundiendo! ¡El BAHR-koh seh ehs-TAH oon-d'YEHN-doh!	The boat is sinking!
¡Hombre al mar! ¡OHM-breh ahl mahr!	Man overboard!
¡Abandonen el barco! ¡Ah-bahn-DOH-nehn el BAHR-koh!	Abandon ship!
¡Bajen las lanchas salvavidas! ¡BAH-hehn lahs LAHN-chahs sahl-bah-BEE-dahs!	Lower the life boats! *

Entramos en el muelle. Ehn-TRAH-mohs ehn el MWEH-yeh.	We're docking. *

BODY PARTS (EL CUERPO)

¿Con qué: With what:
¿Kohn keh:

corres, (las piernas)   do you run, (legs)
KOH-rrehs, (lahs p'YEHR-nahs)

hablas, (la boca)   do you speak, (mouth)
AH-blahs, (lah BOH-kah)

ves, (los ojos)   do you see, (eyes)
behs, (lohs OH-hohs)

te paras en puntas? (los dedos del pie)   do you stand on tiptoe?
teh PAH-rahs ehn POON-tahs?   (toes)
(lohs DEH-dohs dehl p'YEH)

CAMPING (CAMPING)

Voy de camping.   I'm going camping.
Boy deh KAHM-peeng.

Necesitamos una tienda de campaña nueva.   We need a new tent.
Neh-seh-see-TAH-mohs OO-nah t'YEHN-dah
deh kahm-PAH-n'yah n'WEH-bah.

Ésta (f) tiene agujeros.   This one has holes in it.
EHS-tah t'YEH-neh ah-goo-HEHR-ohs.

Me alegre que todavía tenemos el camper.   I am happy that we still
Meh ah-LEH-greh keh toh-dah-BEE-ah   have our camper.
teh-NEH-mohs el KAHM-pehr.

Armemos la tienda de campaña aquí.   Let's pitch the tent here.
Ahr-MEH-mohs lah t'YEHN-dah deh
kahm-PAH-n'yah ah-KEE.

81

Quiero un camping al lado del lago.
K'YEH-roh oon KAHM-peeng ahl LAH-doh
dehl LAH-goh.

I want a campsite right
on the lake.

Monta la hornilla.
MOHN-tah lah ohr-NEE-yah.

Set up the stove.

COLORING and PASTING   (PINTAR y PEGAR)

Déjale usar tus crayones.
DEH-hah-leh oo-SAHR toos krah-
YOHN-ehs.

Let her use your crayons.

Colorea el sol amarillo.
Koh-loh-REH-ah el sohl ah-mah-REE-yoh.

Color the sun yellow.

Pinta el pájaro del color que te guste.
PEEN-tah el PAH-hah-roh dehl koh-LOHR
keh teh GOO-steh.

Paint the bird the color you
like.

Haz un dibujo de papi.
Ahs oon dee-BOO-hoh deh PAH-pee.

Draw a picture of daddy.

Dibuja el círculo, el triángulo, el cuadrado así.
Dee-BOO-hah el SEER-koo-loh, el tree-AHN-
goo-loh, el kwah-DRAH-doh ah-SEE.

Draw the circle, triangle, the
square like this.

Corta este retrato de la revista.
KOHR-tah EHS-teh rreh-TRAH-toh deh
lah rreh-BEES-tah.

Cut out this picture from the
magazine.

Pégalo/la/ en el papel con cuidado. (m/f)
PEH-gah-loh/lah/ ehn el pah-PEHL kohn
kwee-DAH-doh.

Paste it carefully on the paper.

Dobla el papel/en dos partes/ en cuatro partes/.
DOH-blah el pah-PEHL/ehn dohs PAHR-tehs/
ehn KWAH-troh PAHR-tehs/.

Fold the paper /in two/
in four/.

No rompas el papel.
Noh RROHM-pahs el pah-PEHL.

Don't tear the paper.

/Rueda/ forma/ aprieta/ la plasticina así.
RRWEH-dah/ FOHR-mah/ ah-pree-EH-tah/
lah plah-stee-SEE-nah ah-SEE.

/Roll/ form/ squeeze/ the clay.
like this.

Recoje tus pasteles y tu papel.
Rreh-KOH-heh toos pah-STEH-lehs ee
too pah-PEHL.

Clean up your crayons and paper.

COMPUTERS   (COMPUTADORES)

¿Quieres jugar juegos electrónicos?
¿K'YEHR-ehs hoo-GAHR hoo-EH-gohs
eh-lehk-TROHN-ee-kohs?

Do you want to play a computer
game?

Vamos a imprimir el archivo.
BAH-ohs ah eem-pree-MEER el ahr-CHEE-boh.

Let's print the file.

Hay un error electrónico.
Igh oon eh-RROHR eh-lehk-TROHN-ee-koh.

There's a computer error.

¡No borres el archivo!
¡Noh BOH-rrehs el ahr-CHEE-boh!

Don't erase the file!

Quiero usar el explorador.
K'YEH-roh oo-SAHR el ehs-plohr-ah-DOHR.

I want to use the scanner.

DOLLS   (MUÑECAS)

Dale de comer a la muñeca.
DAH-leh deh koh-MEHR ah lah
moo-n'YEH-kah.

Feed the doll.   *

Víste a la muñeca.
BEES-teh ah lah moo-n'YEH-kah.

Dress the doll.

Acuéstala con cuidado.
Ah-KWEHS-tah-lah kohn kwee-DAH-doh.

Lay her down gently.

No la arrastres en el suelo. Noh lah ah-RRAHS-trehs ehn el SWEH-loh.	Don't drag her on the floor.
No le pegues a ella tan fuerte. Noh leh PEH-gehs ah EH-yah tahn FWEHR-teh.	Don't spank her so hard.
¿Cómo se llama la muñeca? ¿KOH-moh seh YAH-mah lah moo-n'YEH-kah?	What is the doll's name?
Tú puedes diseñar una ropa al computador. Too PWEH-dehs dee-sehn-YAHR OO-nah RROH-pah ahl kohm-poo-tah-DOHR.	You can design a dress on the computer.

OBSTACLE GAMES   (JUEGOS de OBSTÁCULOS)

Anda: AHN-dah:	Go:
por el aro, pohr el AH-roh,	through the hoop,
alrededor del gabinete, ahl-reh-deh-DOHR dehl gah-bee-NEH-teh,	around the cabinet,
debajo de la mesa, deh-BAH-hoh deh lah MEH-sah,	under the table,
al lado de la silla. ahl LAH-doh deh lah SEE-yah.	beside the chair.
Párate detrás de mí, delante del sofá. PAH-rah-teh deh-TRAHS deh mee, deh- LAHN-teh dehl soh-FAH.	Stand behind me, in front of the couch.

PLAYGROUND   (PATIO de RECREO)

¡Anda y escóndete! ¡AHN-dah ee ehs-KOHN-deh-teh!	Go and hide!

84

¿Dónde estás? ¿Dónde estoy? ¿DOHN-deh ehs-TAHS? ¿DOHN-deh ehs-TOY?	Where are you? Where am I?
No saltes del columpio. Noh SAHL-tehs dehl koh-LOOM-pee-oh.	Don't jump off the swing.
¡Columpiate! Pero no te columpies demasiado fuerte. ¡Koh-loom-pee-AH-teh! PEH-roh noh teh koh- LOOM-pee-ehs deh-mah-s'-YAH-doh FWEHR-teh.	Swing! But don't swing too high. *
No te pares en el columpio. Noh teh PAH-rehs ehn el koh-LOOM-pee-oh.	Don't stand on the swing.
Te empujaré suavemente. Teh ehm-poo-hah-RAY swah-beh-MEHN-teh.	I'll push you gently.
No cierres los ojos. Noh s'YEH-rrehs lohs OH-hohs.	Don't close your eyes.
Haz cola. Ahz KOH-lah.	Stand in line. (one child)
Agárrate de la resbaladilla Ah-GAH-rrah-teh deh lah rrehs-bah-lah-DEE-yah.	Hold onto the slide. *
Agárrate del carrusel. Ah-GAH-rrah-teh dehl kah-rroo-SEHL.	Hold onto the merry-go-round.
Resbala despacio. Rrehs-BAH-lah dehs-PAH-see-oh.	Slide down gently.
La cometa está cayendo; no hay bastante viento. Lah koh-MEH-tah ehs-TAH kah-YEHN-doh; noh igh bah-STAHN-teh b'YEHN-toh.	The kite is falling; there's not enough wind.
Agarra la cola. Ah-GAH-rrah lah KOH-lah.	Hold onto the tail.

¿Quieres/saltar la cuerda/o jugar con el trompo/?　Do you want/to jump rope/
¿K'YEH-rehs/ sahl-TAHR lah k'WEHR-dah/ oh　or play with the top/?
hoo-GAHR kohn el TROHM-poh/?

Tira las canicas al círculo.　Shoot the marbles into the
TEE-rah las kah-NEE-kahs ahl　circle.
SEER-koo-loh.

Infla el globo. El aire se está saliendo.　Blow up the balloon. Air is
EEN-flah el GLOH-boh. El IGH-reh seh　leaking from it.
ehs-TAH sah-l'YEHN-doh.

QUIET GAMES　(JUEGOS TRANQUILOS)

Jugamos un juego tranquilo.　Let's play a quiet game.
Hoo-GAH-mohs oon hoo-EH-goh
trahn-KEE-loh.

Vamos a poner este pedazo del　Let's put this piece of the
rompecabezas aquí.　puzzle here.
BAH-mohs ah poh-NEHR EHS-teh peh-DAH-
soh dehl rrohm-peh-kah-BEH-sahs ah-KEE.

Este pedazo no cabe.　This piece doesn't fit.
EHS-teh peh-DAH-soh noh KAH-beh.

¿Piensas que este pedazo va aquí?　Do you think this piece
¿P'YEHN-sahs keh EHS-teh peh-DAH-soh　goes here?
bah ah-KEE?

¿Qué pedazo falta?　What piece is missing?
¿Keh peh-DAH-soh FAHL-tah?

Este rompecabezas es demasiado /fácil/ dificil/.　This puzzle is too/ easy/
EHS-teh rrohm-peh-kah-BEH-sahs ehs deh-　difficult/.
mah-s'YAH-doh/ FAH-seel/ deef-EE-seel/.

Mira por la ventana.　Look out the window.
MEE-rah pohr lah behn-TAH-nah.

¿Qué ves? ¿Keh behs?	What do you see?
¡Adivina quién es! ¡Ah-dee-BEE-nah k'YEHN ehs!	Guess who!
Espío con mi ojito algo que... (es color café y alto). (un árbol) Ehs-PEE-oh kohn mee oh-HEE-toh AHL-goh keh... (ehs koh-LOHR kah-FEH ee AHL-toh). (oon AHR-bohl)	I spy with my little eye some- thing that... (is brown and tall). (a tree)
¿Quieres jugar una partida de cartas (conmigo)? ¿K'YEHR-ehs hoo-GAHR OO-nah pahr-TEE- dah deh KAHR-tahs (kohn-MEE-goh)?	Do you want to play a game of cards (with me)?
Puedes revisar tu colección. PWEH-dehs rreh-bee-SAHR too koh-lehk- s'YOHN.	You can sort through your collection.

SKATING   (PATINAR)

Mis patines están desafilados. Necesitan ser afilados. Mees pah-TEE-nehs ehs-TAHN deh-sah-fee- LAH-dohs. Neh-seh-SEE-tahn sehr ah-fee- LAH-dohs.	My skates are dull. They need sharpening. *
Agárrate de mí. Te ayudaré a patinar. Ah-GAH-rrah-teh deh mee. Teh ah-yoo-dah- REH ah pah-tee-NAHR.	Hold on to me. I'll help you skate.
Levanta el pie derecho. Leh-BAHN-tah el p'YEH deh-REH-choh.	Lift your right foot.
Empuja con el pie izquierdo. Ehm-POO-hah kohn el p'YEH ees- k'YEHR-doh.	Push with your left foot.
Patina alrededor de la sala de patinar. Pah-TEE-nah ahl-reh-deh-DOHR deh lah SAH-1ah deh pah-tee-NAHR.	Skate around the rink.

Estás listo/a/ para patinar hacia atrás. (m/f) Ehs-TAHS LEES-toh/tah/ PAH-rah pah-tee- NAHR ah-SEE-ah ah-TRAHS.	You're ready to skate backwards.
Patina solamente en el camino de entrada. Pah-TEE-nah soh-lah-MEHN-teh ehn el kah- MEE-noh deh ehn-TRAH-dah.	Skate only in the driveway.

SOCCER   (FÚTBOL)

No toques la pelota con las manos. Noh TOH-kehs lah peh-LOH-tah kohn lahs MAH-nohs.	Don't touch the ball with your hands. *
Patea la pelota al gol. Pah-TEH-ah lah peh-LOH-tah ahl gohl.	Kick the ball into the goal.
¡Qué salvada! ¡Keh sahl-BAH-dah!	What a great save!
¡Mira cómo gambeteas! ¡MEE-rah KOH-moh gahm-beh-TEH-ahs!	Look at your footwork!
¡Qué /golazo/ foul/ penal/! ¡Keh /goh-LAH-soh/ fowl/ peh-NAHL/!	What a /goal/ foul/ penalty kick/!
Este partido está reñido. EHS-teh pahr-TEE-doh ehs-TAH rreh-n'YEE-doh.	This game is close.
Pasame/ la pelota. PAH-sah-meh/ lah peh-LOH-tah.	Pass /the ball/ to me.
¡Qué buen pase! ¡Keh bwehn PAH-seh!	That was a good pass!
¡Has marcado un gol! ¡Ahs mahr-KAH-doh oon gohl!	You have scored a goal!
El árbitro toca el silbato. El AHR-bee-troh TOH-kah el seel-BAH-toh.	The referee is blowing his whistle.

88

TRAINS and TRUCKS   (TRENES y CAMIONES)

¡Abordo! Boletos, por favor.
¡Ah-BOHR-doh! Boh-LEH-tohs, pohr fah-BOHR.

All aboard! Tickets, please.

¿Cuánto es el pasaje?
¿KWAHN-toh ehs el pah-SAH-heh?

How much is the fare?

¿Cuándo llegamos a Nueva York?
¿KWAHN-doh yeh-GAH-mohs ah
Noo-EH-bah York?

When do we arrive in New York?

¿Repartes aceite en tu camión de aceite?
¿Rreh-PAHR-tehs ah-SEH-teh ehn too kah-
m'YOHN deh ah-SEH-teh?

Are you delivering oil in your
oil truck?

Yo conduzco/hacia atrás/ adelante/.
Yoh kohn-DOOS-koh /ah-SEE-ah ah-TRAHS/
ah-deh-LAHN-teh/.

I'm driving/ backwards/ forwards/.

Este no es un camión de aceite; es una
bomba de incendios.
Ehs-teh noh ehs oon kah-m'YOHN deh ah-
SEH-teh; ehs OO-nah BOHM-bah deh
een-sehn-DEE-ohs.

This is not an oil truck; this is a
fire engine.   *

Quiero una camioneta roja.
K'YEH-roh OO-nah kah-mee-yohn-EH-tah
RROH-hah.

I want a red pick-up.

Estoy cargando mi camión con arena.
Ehs-TOY kahr-GAHN-doh mee kah-m'YOHN
kohn ah-REH-nah.

I'm loading my truck with sand.

Me gusta la caja de quinta.
Meh GOO-stah lah KAH-hah deh KEEN-tah.

I like the five-speed
transmission.

Cuando recibo mi permiso de conducir.......
KWAHN-doh rreh-SEE-boh mee pehr-MEE-
soh deh kohn-doo-SEER...

When I get my driver's license
....

No hay mejor hermano que un buen vecino al lado. Good neighbors are hard to find.

SÁBADO *por* LA TARDE   SATURDAY AFTERNOON

The opportunities for using Spanish on Saturdays are unlimited. Saturdays were made for Spanish! Chores to be done using Spanish, visits to friends using Spanish, shopping, outings, sports. The list is endless as you can see.

Vámonos /a ir al cine/ al centro commercial/.
BAH-moh-nohs /ah eer ahl SEE-neh/
ahl SEHN-troh koh-mehr-s'YAHL/.

Let's go/ see a movie/ to the mall/.

¿Pueden venir_____ y_____con nosotros?
¿PWEH-dehn behn-EER_____ee_____
kohn noh-SOH-trohs?

Can _____and_____
come with us?

Prefiero ir al patio de recreo.
Preh-f'YEH-roh eer ahl PAH-t'yoh
deh rreh-KREH-oh.

I'd rather go to the playground.

Es más divertido.
Ehs mahs dee-behr-TEE-doh.

It's more fun.

Da conmigo /al campo/ a la feria/.
Dah kohn-MEE-goh/ ahl KAHM-poh/
ah la FEH-ree-ah/.

Meet me /at the field/
at the country fair/.

¿Has terminado las faenas?
¿Ahs tehr-mee-NAH-doh lahs fah-EH-nahs?

Are your chores done?

¿Habrá algun buen programa en la tele?
¿Ah-BRAH ahl-GOON bwehn proh-
GRAH-mah ehn lah teh-leh?

Is there anything good on TV?

Mostramos el canal en español.
Moh-STRAH-mohs el kah-NAHL ehn
eh-spah-n'YOHL.

Let's watch the Spanish
channel.

Hay:
Igh:
un espectáculo de trenes,
oon eh-spehk-TAH-koo-loh deh TREH-nehs,

There's:

a train show,   *

una pieza en la escuela,
OO-nah p'YEH-sah ehn lah ehs-k'WEH-lah,

a play at school,

un espectáculo de marionetas,
oon eh-spehk-TAH-koo-loh deh mahr-ee-
oh-NEH-tahs,

a puppet show,

un concierto de música rock.
oon kohn-s'YEHR-toh deh MOO-see-kah
rohk.

a rock concert.

Tomaremos/ el metro/ el autobús/.
Toh-mah-REH-mohs /el meh-TROH/
el ow-toh-BOOS.

We'll take /the subway/
the bus/.

Quiero probar /comida mejicana/
comida rápida/.
K'YEH-roh proh-BAHR /koh-MEE-dah meh-
hee-KAH-nah/ koh-MEE-dah RRAH-pee-dah/.

I want to try /Mexican food/
fast food/.

Tienes una cita con el dentista.
T'YEHN-ehs OO-nah SEE-tah kohn
el dehn-TEES-tah.

You have an appointment at the
dentist's.

¡Lo siento!
¡Loh s'YEHN-toh!

Sorry!

Hay que arreglar los aparatos.
Igh keh ah-rreh-GLAHR lohs ah-pahr-AH-tohs.

Your braces need adjustment.

91

¡No! ¡No puedes teñirte el pelo rojo!
¡No! ¡No PWEH-dehs teh-n'YEER-teh
el PEH-loh RROH-hoh/!

No! You can't get your hair
dyed red!

Súbete y vamos a dar un paseo en coche.
SOO-beh-teh ee BAH-mos ah dahr oon
pah-SEH-oh ehn KOH-cheh.

Hop in, and we'll go for a
ride.

Llama a _____, y vamos de paseo
en monopatín.
YAH-mah ah _____, ee BAH-mohs deh
pah-SEH-oh ehn moh-noh-pah-TEEN.

Call _____ ,and
let's go skateboarding.   *

¡Vuelo libre sería divertido!
¡BWEH-loh LEE-breh seh-REE-ah
dee-behr-TEE-doh!

Hang-gliding would be fun!

Escuchamos el disco compacto.
Ehs-koo-CHAH-mohs el DEES-koh
kohm-PAHK-toh.

Let's listen to the CD.

¿Te gustaría ir a pescar?
¿Teh goo-stahr-EE-ah eer ah pehs-KAHR?

Would you like to go fishing?

Prefiero ir a pescar.
Preh-f'YEH-roh eer ah pehs-KAHR.

I'd rather go fishing.   *

Tenemos el cebo, los anzuels, y la red.
Teh-NEH-mohs el SEH-boh, lohs ahn-soo-
EHLS, ee lah rehd.

We've got the bait, hooks
and net.

Te olvidaste de la caña de pescar.
Teh ohl-bee-DAH-steh deh lah KAH-n'yah
deh pehs-KAHR.

You forgot the fishing rod.

El hilo de pescar está cogido al fondo.
El EE-loh deh pehs-KAHR ehs-TAH
koh-HEE-doh ahl FOHN-doh.

My fishing line is caught on
the bottom.

¡Cogí dos peces!
¡Koh-HEE dohs PEH-sehs!

I caught two fish!

¿Podemos construir la casita en el árbol?
¿Poh-DEH-mohs kohn-stroo-EER lah
kah-SEE-tah ehn el AHR-bohl?

Can we build the tree house?

Da conmigo en el jardín trasero.
Dah kohn-MEE-goh ehn el hahr-DEEN
trah-SEH-roh.

Meet me in the back yard.

Vamos a:
BAH-mohs ah:

Let's:

    ir al desván,
    eer ahl dehs-BAHN,

    go to the attic,

    mirar/dibujos animados/ fútbol/
    en la televisión,
    mee-RAHR/ dee-BOO-hohs ah-nee-
    MAH-dohs/ FOOT-bohl/ ehn lah
    teh-leh-bee-s'YOHN,

    watch/cartoons/ soccer/
    on TV,

    leer las cómicas,
    leh-EHR lahs KOH-mee-kahs,

    read comics,

    alquilar un vídeo,
    ahl-kee-LAHR oon BEE-deh-yoh,

    rent a video,

    ir/ a la playa/ al lago/,
    eer/ ah lah PLAH-yah/ ahl LAH-goh/,

    go to the / beach/ lake/,

    ir/ al océano/ a la piscina/,
    eer/ ahl oh-SEH-ah-noh/ ah lah pee-SEE-nah/,

    go to the /ocean/ pool/,

    nadar,
    nah-DAHR,

    go swimming,

    esquiar en agua.
    ehs-kee-AHR ehn AH-gwah.

    go waterskiing.

Llevo:
Yeh-BOH:

I'll bring:

    mis discos compactos,
    mees DEES-kohs kohm-PAHK-tohs,

    my CD's,

las toallas,
lahs toh-AH-yahs,

the towels,

la sombrilla,
lah sohm-BREE-yah,

the beach umbrella,

la silla de la playa,
lah SEE-yah deh lah PLAH-yah,

the beach chair,

el balde y la pala.
el BAHL-deh ee lah PAH-lah.

the shovel and the pail. *

¡Todos afuera!
¡TOH-dohs ah-FWEHR-ah!

Everybody out!

¡Aquí estamos!
¡Ah-KEE ehs-TAH-mohs!

Here we are!

Vamos a quedarnos aquí. No hay
demasiada gente.
BAH-mohs ah keh-DAHR-nohs ah-KEE.
Noh igh deh-mah-s'YAH-dah HEHN-teh.

Let's stay here. There aren't
too many people.

Prefiero la sombra.
Preh-f'YEH-roh lah SOHM-brah.

I prefer the shade.

Está cerca del /agua/ puesto de bebidas/.
Ehs-TAH SEHR-kah dehl/ AH-gwah/
PWEHS-toh deh beh-BEE-dahs/.

It's near the /water/ drink
stand/.

El agua parece clara.
El AH-gwah pah-REH-seh KLAH-rah.

The water looks clear.

¡Mira las olas!
¡MEE-rah lahs OH-lahs!

Look at the waves!

¡El mar está revuelto!
¡El mahr ehs-TAH rreh-BWEHL-toh!

The sea is rough!

¿Por qué no recojes algunas conchas
de mar?
¿Pohr KEH noh rreh-KOH-hehs
ahl-GOO-nahs KOHN-chahs deh mahr?

Why don't you collect some
seashells? *

94

No puedes meterte al agua ahora.
Acabas de almorzar.
Noh PWEH-dehs meh-TEHR-teh ahl
AH-gwah ah-OH-rah. Ah-KAH-bahs
deh ahl-mohr-SAHR.

You can't go into the water
now. You have just eaten lunch.

Ese bote de carrera está muy cerca
de la boya.
EH-seh BOH-teh deh kah-RREH-rah ehs-
TAH mwee SEHR-kah deh lah BOH-yah.

That speed boat is very close
to the buoy.   *

Flota boca arriba.
FLOH-tah BOH-kah ah-RREE-bah.

Float on your back.

Sal del agua.
Sahl dehl AH-gwah.

Come out of the water.

Estás temblando del frío.
Ehs-TAHS tehm-BLAHN-doh dehl
FREE-oh.

You're shivering with cold.

Hay algas en tu espalda.
Igh AHL-gahs ehn too ehs-PAHL-dah.

There's seaweed on your
back.

Haz un castillo de arena.
Ahs oon kah-STEE-yoh deh ah-REH-nah.

Build a sand castle.   *

No te sientes en el sol por demasiado tiempo.
Noh teh s'YEHN-tehs ehn el sohl pohr
deh-mah-s'YAH-doh t'YEHM-poh.

Don't sit in the sun too long.

No te quemes con el sol.
Noh teh KEH-mehs kohn el sohl.

You must not get sunburnt.

¿Dónde está la bloqueadora?
¿DOHN-deh ehs-TAH lah bloh-keh-ah-
DOHR-ah?

Where is the sun block?

Quiero asolearme.
K'YEH-roh ah-soh-leh-AHR-meh.

I want to get a suntan.

El sol está/ fuerte/ caliente/.
El sohl ehs-TAH/ FWEHR-teh/ kah-l'YEHN-teh/.

The sun is / strong/ hot/.

95

Mira los pájaros/ bajar/ volar/.
MEE-rah lohs PAH-hah-rohs/
bah-HAHR/ boh-LAHR/.

Watch the birds/ come down/ fly/.

¿Te olvidaste de los anteojos de sol?
¿Teh ohl-bee-DAHS-teh deh lohs
ahn-teh-OH-hohs deh sohl?

Did you forget your sunglasses?　　*

¿Cuándo salimos?
¿KWAHN-doh sah-LEE-mohs?

When are we leaving?

Es hora de irnos.
Ehs OH-rah deh EER-nohs.

It's time to go.

Empaquemos.
Ehm-pah-KEH-mohs.

Let's pack up.

Lo pasé bien (en la playa).
Loh pah-SEH b'YEHN (ehn lah PLAH-yah).

I had a good time (at at the beach).

¡Qué te diviertas!
¡Keh teh dee-b'YEHR-tahs!

Have a good time!

Es un placer ir a la playa.
Ehs oon plah-SEHR eer ah lah PLAH-yah.

It's a pleasure to go to the beach.

Vigila a tu hermana.
Bee-HEE-lah ah too ehr-MAH-nah.

Keep an eye on your sister.

Quiero alquilar...
K'YEH-roh ahl-kee-LAHR...

I want to rent...

Necesitamos alquilar palos de esquiar,
esquíes, y botas.
Neh-seh-see-TAH-mohs ahl-kee-LAHR
PAH-lohs deh ehs-k'YAHR,
ehs-KEE-ehs, ee BOH-tahs.

We need to rent ski poles, skis, and boots.　　*

¿Son cómodas tus botas?
¿Sohn KOH-moh-dahs toos BOH-tahs?

Are your boots comfortable?

¿Son demasiado/ largos/ cortos/ tus
palos de esquiar?
¿Sohn deh-mah-s'YAH-doh/LAHR-gohs/
KOHR-tohs/ toos PAH-1ohs deh ehs-k'YAHR?

Are your ski poles too/ long/
short?

Tus tiras de esquiar están demasiado/
sueltas/ apretadas/.
Toos TEE-rahs deh ehs-k'YAHR ehs-TAHN deh-
mah-s'YAH-doh/ SWEHL-tahs/ah-preh-TAH-dahs/.

Your bindings are too/ loose/
tight/.

¿Dónde venden boletos para el telesquí?
¿DOHN-deh BEHN-dehn boh-LEH-tohs
PAH-rah el tehl-eh-SKEE?

Where do they sell tickets for
the ski lift?

No vayas al pico de la montaña.
Noh BAH-yahs ahl PEE-koh deh lah
mohn-TAHN-yah.

Don't go to the top of the hill.

Esa colina es un poco empinada.
EH-sah koh-LEE-nah ehs oon POH-koh
ehm-pee-NAH-dah.

That hill is a little steep.

Aquellos esquiadores van demasiado rápido.
Ah-KEH-yohs ehs-kee-ah-DOH-rehs bahn
deh-mah-s'YAH-doh RRAH-pee-doh.

Those skiers go too fast.

¡Cuidado!
¡Kwee-DAH-doh!

Look out!

No esquíes /demasiado/tanto/ rápido.
Noh ehs-KEE-ehs /deh-mah-s'YAH-doh/
/TAHN-toh/ RRAH-pee-doh.

Don't ski /too/ so/ fast.

La nieve es/suave/dura/.
Lah n'YEH-beh ehs/SWAH-beh/DOO-rah/.

The snow is/soft/ hard/.

¡Qué forma!
¡Keh FOHR-mah!

What form!

Estás esquiando muy bien.
Ehs-TAHS ehs-k'YAHN-doh mwee b'YEHN.

You are skiing just fine.

¿Estás cansado/a/? (m/f)
¿Ehs-TAHS kahn-SAH-doh/dah/?

Are you tired?

¿Tienes/ hambre/ frío/?
¿T'YEH-nehs / AHM-breh/ FREE-oh/?

Are you/ hungry/ cold/?

Tengo /hambre/ frío/.
TEHN-goh/ AHM-breh/ FREE/oh/.

I'm / hungry/ cold/.

Vamos adentro a/ descansar/ comer/
calentarnos/.
BAH-mohs ah-DEHN-troh ah/ dehs-kahn-
SAHR/ koh-MEHR/ kah-lehn-TAHR-nohs/.

Let's go inside to/ rest/ eat/
warm up/.

Ven a calentarte.
Behn ah kah-lehn-TAHR-teh.

Come warm yourself.

Aquí hace un calorcito muy agradable.
Ah-KEE AH-seh oon kah-lorh-SEE-toh
mwee ah-grah-DAH-bleh.

It's nice and warm here.

Va a haber mucho tráfico.
Bah ah ah-BEHR MOO-choh TRAH-fee-koh.

There is going to be a lot of
traffic.

No olvides cualquier cosa.
Noh ohl-BEE-dehs kwal-kee-EHR KOH-sah.

Don't forget anything.

¿Te olvidaste algo?
¿Teh ohl-bee-DAH-steh AHL-goh?

Did you forget something?

Llama a tus padres.
YAH-mah ah toos PAH-drehs.

Call your parents.

Están esperando que los llames.
Ehs-TAHN ehs-pehr-AHN-doh keh
lohs YAH-mehs.

They are waiting for you
to call them.

¿Te divertiste?
¿Teh dee-behr-TEE-steh?

Did you have a good time?

98

¡Le has tocado el gordo! You hit the jackpot!

EXCLAMACIONES	EXCLAMATIONS

¡Ay!
¡Igh!

Ah! Wow! Ouch! Whoops!

¡Caramba!
¡Kah-RAHM-bah!

Darn! Wow!

¡Se me olvidó por completo!
¡Seh meh ohl-bee-DOH pohr kohm-PLEH-toh!

It completely slipped my mind!

Me alegro. (or) Estoy alegre.
Meh ah-LEH-groh. (or) Ehs-TOY ah-LEH-greh.

I am glad.

Estamos contentos/as de que hayas ganado. (m/f)
Ehs-TAH-mohs kohn-TEHN-tohs/ tahs deh
keh AH-yahs gah-NAH-doh.

We are glad that you won.

Estoy triste.
Ehs-TOY TREES-teh.

I am sad.

¡Socorro!
¡Soh-KOH-rroh!

Help!

¡Cuidado!
¡Kwee-DAH-doh!

Look out! Go easy!

Lo siento. Es mi culpa.　　　　　　　　　I'm sorry. It's my fault.
Loh s'YEHN-toh. Ehs mee KOOL-pah.

Es culpa tuya.　　　　　　　　　　　　　It's your fault.
Ehs KOOL-pah TOO-yah.

No entendí todo lo que me dijiste.　　　　I didn't understand
Noh ehn-tehn-DEE toh-doh loh keh meh　　everything you said.
dee-HEES-teh.

¡No me hagas acordar!　　　　　　　　　Don't remind me!
¡Noh meh AH-gahs ah-kohr-DAHR!

Siento que hayas caído.　　　　　　　　I'm sorry that you fell.
See-EHN-toh keh AH-yahs kah-EE-doh.

¡Pues bien!　　　　　　　　　　　　　Well now!
¡Pwehs b'YEHN!

¿No es verdad? ¿Verdad?　　　　　　　Isn't that so? Is that so?
¿Noh ehs behr-DAHD? ¿Behr-DAHD?

¿A quién le importa?　　　　　　　　　Who cares?
¿Ah k'YEHN leh eem-POHR-tah?

No me importa.　　　　　　　　　　　I don't care.
Noh meh eem-POHR-tah.

No importa.　　　　　　　　　　　　It doesn't matter.
Noh eem-POHR-tah.

¿Quién sabe?　　　　　　　　　　　Who knows?
¿K'YEHN SAH-beh?

Bueno. Está bien.　　　　　　　　　Okay. All right.
BWEH-noh. Ehs-TAH b'YEHN.

¡Por supuesto!　　　　　　　　　　Of course!
¡Pohr soo-PWEHS-toh!

¡Claro que no!　　　　　　　　　　Of course not!
¡KLAH-roh keh noh!

¡Ciertamente! ¡Seguro! ¡S'YEHR-tah-mehn-teh! ¡Seh-GOO-roh!	Certainly! Sure!
¡Sin duda! ¡Seen DOO-dah!	Without fail!
¡De ninguna manera! ¡Deh neen-GOON-ah mah-NEHR-ah!	No way!
¡Qué interesante! ¡Keh een-teh-reh-SAHN-teh!	How interesting!
¡Qué divertido! Es cómico. ¡Keh dee-behr-TEE-doh! Ehs KOH-mee-koh.	How funny! It's funny.
¡Qué tontería! ¡Keh tohn-teh-REE-ah!	What nonsense!
¡Qué cosa! ¡Keh KOH-sah!	Good grief!
No estoy para bromas. Noh ehs-TOY PAH-rah BROH-mahs.	I'm not in the mood for jokes.
¡Qué suerte! ¡Keh SWEHR-teh!	What luck! *
¡Tienes suerte! ¡T'YEHN-ehs SWEHR-teh!	You are lucky!
¡Qué horrible! ¡Keh oh-RREE-bleh!	How awful!
¡Qué lástima! ¡Keh LAHS-tee-mah!	Too bad! What a pity!
¡Qué raro! ¡Es extraordinario! ¡Keh RRAH-roh! ¡Ehs ehs-trah-ohr-dee- NAH-ree-oh!	How unusual! That's extraordinary!
¡Qué simpatico/a/! (m/f) ¡Keh seem-PAH-tee-koh/ kah/!	How kind/ nice!

101

¡Maravilloso!
¡Mah-rah-bee-YOH-soh!

Marvelous! Wonderful!

¡Me salvas la vida!
¡Meh SAHL-bahs lah BEE-dah!

You saved my life!

¡Eres el mejor!
¡EH-rehs el meh-HOHR!

You're the greatest!

¡Qué chiste!
¡Keh CHEES-teh!

What a joke!

¡Claro que sí!
¡KLAH-roh keh see!

I should say so!

¡Es imposible!
¡Ehs eem-poh-SEE-bleh!

It's out of the question!

¡No puede ser!
¡Noh PWEH-deh sehr!

It's impossible! It can't be!

No te preocupes.
Noh teh preh-oh-KOO-pehs.

Don't worry.

Le podría pasar a cualquiera.
Leh poh-DREE-ah pah-SAHR ah
kwahl-k'YEHR-ah.

It could happen to anyone.

Está bien.
Ehs-TAH b'YEHN.

It's all right. That's fine.

No es correcto. No es justo.
Noh ehs koh-RREHK-toh. Noh ehs HOOS-toh.

It's not right. It's not fair.

¡Aquí hay gato encerrado!
¡Ah-KEE igh GAH-toh ehn-seh-RRAH-doh!

I smell a rat!
(There's a hidden cat here.)

¡Eso es!
¡EH-soh ehs!

That's it!

No es necesario.
Noh ehs neh-seh-SAH-ree-oh.

That is not necessary.

¡Todo terminado!
¡TOH-doh tehr-mee-NAH-doh!

All gone!

¡Upah!
¡OO-pah!

Up you go!

¡Mira qué desorden!
¡MEE-rah keh deh-SOHR-dehn!

Look at the mess!

¡Es verdad! ¿Es verdad?
¡Ehs behr-DAHD! ¿Ehs behr-DAHD?

That's true! Is that so?

¡Espero que /sí/ no/!
¡Eh-SPEH-roh keh /see/ noh/!

I hope /so/ not/!

¡Creo que /sí/ no/!
¡KREH-oh keh /see/noh/!

I think /so/ not/!

Pues . . . Entonces... A ver...
PWEHS... Ehn-TOHN-sehs...
Ah behr...

Well... Then... Let me see...
(an expression of hesitation
while considering a reply)

¡Ahora bien!
¡Ah-OH-rah b'YEHN!

Well now!

¡De veras! ¡No me digas!
¡Deh BEH-rahs! ¡Noh meh DEE-gahs!

Indeed! You don't say!

¿Qué?
¿Keh?

What?

Como siempre...
KOH-moh see-YEHM-preh...

As usual. . .

¡Qué estornudo! ¡Salud!
¡Keh ehs-tohr-NOO-doh! ¡Sah-LOOD!

What a sneeze! God bless you!

¡Qué mala cara pones!
¡Keh MAH-lah KAH-rah POH-nehs!

How you frown!

103

¿Qué pasa?
¿Keh PAH-sah?

What is wrong?

¿Qué te pasa?
¿Keh teh PAH-sah?

What is the matter with you?

¿Por qué /te quejas/ estás enojado/a?
¿Pohr KEH /teh KEH-hahs/ ehs-TAHS
ehn-oh-HAH-doh/dah/?

Why are you /complaining/
angry/?

¡Por Dios!
¡Pohr dee-OHS!

For goodness sake!

¡Esto no es para reírte!
¡EHS-toh noh ehs PAH-rah rreh-EER-teh!

This is no laughing matter!

¡Lo mereces!
¡Loh meh-REH-sehs!

It serves you right!

¡No debes decir eso!
¡Noh DEH-behs deh-SEER EH-soh!

You must not say that!

¡Dios me ampare!
¡Dee-OHS meh ahm-PAH-reh!

God forbid!

¡Por el amor de Dios!
¡Pohr el ah-MOHR deh dee-OHS!

Why on earth!

¡Es inmenso/a/! (m/f)
¡Ehs een-MEHN-soh/sah/!

It's immense!

¡Está bien!
¡Ehs-TAH b'YEHN!

That's fine!

Déjalo.
DEH-hah-loh.

Stop it.

Ve y sé feliz.
Beh ee seh feh-LEES.

Go and be happy.

No dejes para mañana lo que puedas hacer hoy. **Never put off tomorrow what you can do today.**

FIESTA de CUMPLEAÑOS

BIRTHDAY PARTY

¿Qué te gustaría para tu cumpleaños?
¿Keh teh goo-stah-REE-ah PAH-rah too koom-pleh-AHN-yohs?

What would you like for your birthday?

¿Te gustaría tener una fiesta:
¿Teh goo-stah-REE-ah teh-NEHR OO-nah f'YEHS-tah:

Would you like to have a party:

en casa,
ehn KAH-sah,

at home,

en un restaurante,
ehn oon rehs-tow-RAHN-teh,

at a restaurant,

en el parque,
ehn el PAHR-keh,

at the park,

o a la playa?
oh ah lah PLAH-yah?

or at the beach?

Invitaremos a tus amigos/as/. (m/f)
Een-bee-tah-REH-mohs ah toos ah-MEE-gohs/ gahs/.

We'll invite your friends.

Tendremos un pastel, helado, sombreritos, juegos y regalos.
Tehn-DREH-mohs oon pahs-TEHL, eh-LAH-doh, sohm-breh-REE-tohs, hoo-EH-gohs, ee rreh-GAH-lohs.

We will have cake, ice cream, hats, games and presents. ٭

¿Cuántos años tienes?
¿KWAHN-tohs AH-n'yohs t'YEH-nehs?

How old are you?

Tengo cinco años.
TEHN-goh SEEN-koh AH-n'yohs.

I am five years old.

No sé.
Noh seh.

I don't know.

Yo nací ...(el 5 de octubre)
Yoh nah-SEE...(el SEEN-koh deh okh-TOO-breh)

I was born...(October 5th)

Sopla las velitas del pastel.
SOH-plah lahs beh-LEE-tahs dehl pahs-TEHL.

Blow out the candles of the cake. ٭

Qué bonita felicitación de cumpleaños.
Keh boh-NEE-tah feh-lee-see-tah-s'YOHN deh koom-pleh-AH-nyohs.

What a pretty birthday card.

Corta la torta de cumpleaños.
KOHR-tah lah TOHR-tah deh koom-pleh-AH-nyohs.

Cut the birthday cake.

Divide el pastel en ocho pedazos.
Dee-BEE-deh el pahs-TEHL ehn OH-choh peh-DAH-sohs.

Divide the cake into eight pieces.

¡Qué buena fiesta!
¡Keh b'WEH-nah f'YEHS-tah!

What a nice party!

106

Mañana será otra día. Tomorrow is another day.

HORA *de* ACOSTARSE   BEDTIME

This may be the hardest part of the day to carry out your foreign language program. You're tired. The children are tired. Suggestion: Memorize some nursery rhymes, poetry and by all means, prayers, to tuck your little one into bed for the night.

¡Qué bostezo!   What a yawn!
¡Keh bohs-TEH-soh!

Estás /bostezando/ cansado/a/? (m/f)   You are /yawning/ tired/?
Ehs-TAHS/ boh-steh-SAHN-doh/ kahn-
SAH-doh/dah/?

Es hora de irse a la cama.   It's time for bed.
Ehs OH-rah deh EER-seh ah lah KAH-mah.

¿Tienes sueño?   Are you sleepy?
¿T'YEHN-nehs SWEHN-yoh?

Te estoy acostando.   I am putting you to bed.
Teh ehs-TOY ah-koh-STAHN-doh.

¿Quieres que yo te acueste?   Do you want me to put you
¿K'YEH-rehs keh yoh teh ah-KWEHS-teh?   to bed?

Busca tu libro.
BOOS-kah too LEE-broh.

Te leeré un cuento antes de que te acuestes.
Teh leh-eh-REH oon KWEHN-toh AHN-tehs
deh keh teh ah-KWEHS-tehs.

Voy por mi libro.
Boy pohr mee LEE-broh.

¿Tienes permiso para mirar la televisión?
¿T'YEH-nehs pehr-MEE-soh PAH-rah
mee-RAHR lah teh-leh-bee-s'YOHN?

Encuentro este programa un tanto aburrido.
Ehn-KWEHN-troh EHS-teh proh-GRAHM-ah
oon TAHN-toh ah-boo-RREE-doh.

Quítate la ropa.
KEE-tah-teh lah RROH-pah.

Ponte las pijamas.
POHN-teh lahs pee-HAH-mahs.

Cuelga la camisa en la percha.
KWEHL-gah lah kah-MEE-sah ehn lah
PEHR-chah.

Guarda toda la ropa.
GWAHR-dah TOH-dah lah RROH-pah.

Estos calcetines necesitan ser lavados.
EHS-tohs kahl-seh-TEE-nehs neh-seh-SEE-
tahn sehr lah-BAH-dohs.

¿Estás listo/a/ para la cama? (m/f)
¿Ehs-TAHS LEES-toh/tah/ PAH-rah
lah KAH-mah?

Go get your book.

I'll read you a story before
you go to bed.

I'll go get my book.

Do you have permission to
watch television?

I find this program a little
boring.

Take off your clothes.

Put on your pajamas.   *

Hang your shirt on the hanger.

Put all your clothes away.

These socks need laundering.

Are you ready for bed?

Dile, "buenas noches" a papi.
DEE-leh,"b'WEH-nahs NOH-chehs"ah PAH-pee.

Say "Goodnight," to daddy.

¿Dijiste las oraciónes?
¿Dee-HEES-teh lahs oh-rah-s'YOH-nehs?

Did you say your prayers?

Estás pesado.
Ehs-TAHS peh-SAH-doh.

You are heavy.

Cierra los ojos. Duérmete.
S'YEH-rrah lohs OH-hohs. DWEHR-meh-teh.

Close your eyes. Go to sleep.

Estate tranquilo. Estate quieto.
Ehs-TAH-teh trahn-KEE-loh. Ehs-TAH-teh
k'YEH-toh.

Be still. Be quiet.

Que duermas bien.
Keh DWEHR-mahs b'YEHN.

Sleep well.

Tienes que dormir ahora.
T'YEH-nehs keh dohr-MEER ah-OH-rah.

You have to sleep now.

Que duermas con los angelitos.
Keh d'WEHR-mahs kohn lohs ahn-heh-
LEE-tohs.

Pleasant dreams. (Sleep with
little angels.)

Tienes que quedarte en la cama.
T'YEH-nehs keh keh-DAHR-teh ehn
lah KAH-mah.

You must stay in bed.

¿No estás en la cama todavía?
¿Noh ehs-TAHS ehn lah KAH-mah
toh-dah-BEE-ah?

You are not in bed yet?

No es demasiado temprano para acostarte.
Noh ehs deh-mah-s'YAH-doh tehm-PRAH-noh
PAH-rah ah-koh-STAHR-teh.

It is not too early to go
to bed.

¿Quieres la luz prendida?
¿K'YEH-rehs lah loos prehn-DEE-dah?

Do you want the light lit?

Mami te quiere.
MAH-mee teh k'YEH-reh.

Mommy loves you.

Dame un beso.
DAH-meh oon BEH-soh.

Give me a kiss.

Dios te bendiga.
Dee-OHS teh behn-DEE-gah.

God bless you.

¿Estás mojado/a/? (m/f)
¿Ehs-TAHS moh-HAH-doh/ dah/?

Are you wet?

¿Estás /despierto/a/ dormido/a/? (m/f)
¿Ehs-TAHS dehs-p'YEHR-toh/ tah/?
¿Ehs-TAHS dohr-MEE-doh/dah?

Are you /awake/ asleep/?

/Ella/ Él/ está durmiendo.
/EH-yah/ El/ ehs-TAH duhr-m'YEHN-doh.

/She/ He/ is sleeping.

¿Por qué no estás dormido/a/ todavía? (m/f)
¿Pohr KEH noh ehs-TAHS dohr-MEE-doh/
dah/ toh-dah-BEE-ah?

Why are you not yet asleep?

¿No puedes dormirte?
¿Noh p'WEH-dehs dohr-MEER-teh?

Can't you fall asleep?

No/ lo/ la/ despiertes. (m/f)
Noh /loh/ lah/ dehs-p'YEHR-tehs.

Don't wake/ him/ her/.

¿Qué quieres, mi hijito/a/? (m/f)
¿Keh k'YEH-rehs, mee ee-HEE-toh/tah/?

What do you want,
my little one?

Te raspaste la cara cuando estabas dormido.
Teh rrahs-PAHS-teh lah KAH-rah KWAHN-
doh ehs-TAH-bahs dohr-MEE-doh.

You scratched your face
in your sleep.

¿Te desangras? Me desangro.
¿Teh deh-SAHN-grahs? Meh deh-SAHN-groh.

Are you bleeding?
I'm bleeding.

¿No te sientes bien?
¿Noh teh s'YEHN-tehs b'YEHN?

Don't you feel well?

¿Estás /mareado/a/ enfermo/a/? (m/f)
¿Ehs-TAHS /mah-reh-AH-doh/dah/
ehn-FEHR-moh/mah/?

Are you /dizzy/ sick/?

Tienes /fiebre/ la gripe/.
T'YEH-nehs /f'YEH-breh/ lah GREE-peh/.

You have /a fever/ the flu/.

Tienes manchitas en el pecho. (Varicela)
TYEH-nehs mahn-CHEE-tahs ehn el
PEH-choh. (Bah-ree-SEH-lah)

You have spots on your chest.
(Chicken pox)

Tus glándulas están hinchadas.
Toos GLAHN-d'lahs ehs-TAHN een-CHAH-dahs.

Your glands are swollen.

Saca la lengua.
SAH-kah lah LEHN-gwah.

Stick out your tongue.

Tienes un resfriado. Estás tosiendo.
T'YEH-nehs oon rrehs-free-YAH-doh.
Ehs-TAHS toh-s'YEHN-doh.

You have a cold. You're
coughing.

Necesitas algo para la tos.
Neh-seh-SEE-tahs AHL-goh PAH-rah lah tohs.

You'll need something for
that cough.

Tapate la boca cuando toses.
Tah-PAH-teh lah BOH-kah k'WAHN-doh
TOH-sehs.

Cover your mouth when
you cough.

Mañana tendrás que guardar cama.
Mahn-YAH-nah tehn-DRAHS keh gwahr-
DAHR KAH-mah.

Tomorrow you'll have to
stay in bed.

¿Te duele/el brazo/el pie/?
¿Teh d'WEH-leh/ el BRAH-soh/el p'YEH/?

Does your/ arm/ foot/ hurt?

¿Quieres una curita (para el dedo)?
¿K'YEH-rehs OO-nah koo-REE-tah?

Do you want a bandaid (for
your finger)?

Un día es un día. It's just one of those things.

EL TIEMPO   WEATHER

Everybody talks about it. Now you and your child can talk about it in Spanish. Try sharing a picture book on weather with your child and discuss the pictures using Spanish. This could be more of a "school" kind of chapter if you and your child want to play school. Flash cards to make, maps to draw, temperatures to record... Fun to be had!

Ya está claro.   It's light.
Yah ehs-TAH KLAH-roh.

Hace sol.   It's sunny.
AH-seh sohl.

No hay nubes.   There are no clouds.
Noh igh NOO-behs.

Brilla el sol.   The sun is shining.
BREE-yah el sohl.

Hace/ mucho calor/ calor/ hoy.   It's/ hot/ warm / today.
AH-seh/ MOO-choh kah-LOHR/kah-LOHR/oy.

Hace un calor terrible. Es verano.   It's terribly hot. It's summer.
AH-seh oon kah-LOHR teh-RREE-bleh.
Ehs beh-RAHN-oh.

Tenemos una ola de calor.
Teh-NEH-mohs OO-nah OH-1ah deh
kah-LOHR.

We're having a heat wave.

No hay ni un respiro de viento.
Noh igh nee oon rreh-SPEE-roh deh
b'YEHN-toh.

There's not even a breath of
wind.

Hace (mucho) viento.
AH-seh (MOO-choh) b'YEHN-toh.

It's (very) windy.

Qué linda noche.
Keh LEEN-dah NOH-cheh.

What a beautiful night.

Hace/ fresco/ frío/.
AH-seh/ FREHS-koh/ FREE-oh/.

It's/ cool/ cold/.

Necesitas un/ abrigo/ suéter/.
Neh-seh-SEE-tahs oon/ ah-BREE-goh/
SWEH-tehr/.

You need a/ coat/ sweater/.

Está (medio) nublado.
Ehs-TAH (MEH-dee-yoh) noo-BLAH-doh.

It's (sort of) cloudy.   *

Llueve. (or) Está lloviendo.
Yoo-EH-beh. (or) Ehs-TAH yoh-b'YEHN-doh.

It's raining.

Está cayendo un chaparrón.
Ehs-TAH kah-YEHN-doh oon chah-
pah-RROHN.

It's pouring (cats and dogs).

Gotas de lluvia están cayendo.
GOH-tahs de YOO-b'yah ehs-TAHN
kah-YEHN-doh.

Raindrops are falling.

Mira la lluvia.
MEE-rah lah YOO-b'yah.

Look at the rain.

La calle está llena de charcos.
Lah KAH-yeh ehs-TAH YEH-nah deh
CHAHR-kohs.

The street is full of puddles.

113

Quítate los zapatos.
KEE-tah-teh lohs sah-PAH-tohs.

Take off your shoes.

Tus pies están mojados.
Toos p'YEHS ehs-TAHN moh-HAH-dohs.

Your feet are wet.

Qué día féo.
Keh DEE-ah FEH-oh.

What an unpleasant day.

Qué mal tiempo.
Keh mahl t'YEHM-poh.

What awful weather.

¡Qué tiempo horrible!
¡Keh t'YEHM-poh oh-RREE-bleh!

What nasty weather!

El tiempo está malo.
El t'YEHM-poh ehs-TAH MAH-loh.

The weather is bad.

Pronto va a estar oscuro.
PROHN-toh bah ah ehs-TAHR ohs-KOO-roh.

It will be dark soon.

Está oscureciendo.
Ehs-TAH ohs-koo-reh-s'YEHN-doh.

It's getting dark.

El cielo está /oscuro/ gris/.
El s'YEH-loh ehs-TAH/ohs-KOO-roh/ grees/.

The sky is/ dark/ gray/.

Hay truenos y relámpagos.
Igh troo-EH-nohs ee rreh-LAHM-pah-gohs.

There's thunder and lightning. *

¡Qué tormenta!
¡Keh tohr-MEHN-tah!

What a storm!

¡Qué niebla! (or) ¡Qué neblina!
¡Keh n'YEH-blah! (or) ¡Keh neh-BLEE-nah!

What fog!

Espera hasta que pare la lluvia.
Ehs-PEH-rah AHS-tah keh PAH-reh lah
YOO-b'yah.

Wait until the rain stops.

¡Mira (el arcoiris)!
¡MEE-rah (el ahr-koh-EE-rees)!

Look (at the rainbow)!

114

Es un verdadero día de invierno.
Ehs oon behr-dah-DEH-roh DEE-ah deh
een-b'YEHR-noh.

It's a real winter day.

Está empezando a nevar.
Ehs-TAH ehm-peh-SAHN-doh ah neh-BAHR.

It's beginning to snow.

Está nevando. (or) Nieva.
Ehs-TAH neh-BAHN-doh.(or) N'YEH-bah.

It's snowing.

Copitos de nieve están cayendo.
Koh-PEE-tohs deh n'YEH-beh ehs-TAHN
kah-YEHN-doh.

Snowflakes are falling.

Mira la nieve.
MEE-rah lah n'YEH-beh.

Look at the snow.

¡Cómo brilla la nieve!
¡KOH-moh BREE-yah lah n'YEH-beh!

How the snow sparkles!

¿Quizás podemos hacer un hombre de nieve?
¿Kee-SAHS poh-DEH-mohs ah-SEHR oon
OHM-breh deh n'YEH-beh?

Perhaps we can make a
snowman?

Ha dejado/ de nevar/ de llover/.
Ah deh-HAH-doh/ deh neh-BAHR/ deh
yoh-BEHR/.

The/snow/rain/has stopped.

La nieve se está descongelando.
Lah n'YEH-beh seh ehs-TAH dehs-kohn-
heh-LAHN-doh.

The snow is melting.

Qué lindo día.
Keh LEEN-doh DEE-ah.

What a beautiful day.

115

Más vale tarde que nunca. Better late than never.

LA HORA

TIME

Es la una.
Ehs lah OO-nah.

It's one o'clock.

Son las dos.
Sohn lahs dohs.

It's two o'clock.

Son las tres y cuarto.
Sohn lahs trehs ee KWAHR-toh.

It's three fifteen.

Son las cuatro y media.
Sohn lahs KWAH-troh ee MEH-dee-ah.

It's four thirty.

Son las cinco menos cuarto.
Sohn lahs SEEN-koh MEH-nohs KWAHR-toh.

It's four forty-five.

Son las seis y veinte.
Sohn lahs SEH-ees ee BAIN-teh.

It's six twenty.

Son las siete menos veinte.
Sohn lahs s'YEH-teh MEH-nohs BAIN-teh.

It's six forty.

Son las ocho.
Sohn lahs OH-choh.

It's eight o'clock.

116

Son las nueve.
Sohn lahs NWEH-beh.

It's nine o'clock.

Son las diez.
Sohn lahs d'YEHS.

It's ten o'clock.

Son las once.
Sohn lahs OHN-seh.

It's eleven o'clock.

Es la medianoche.
Ehs lah meh-d'yah-NOH-cheh.

It's midnight.

Es el mediodía.
Ehs el meh-d'yoh-DEE-ah.

It's noon.

Es de manaña.
Ehs deh mah-n'YAH-nah.

It's morning.

Es de tarde.
Ehs deh TAHR-deh.

It's afternoon.

Es de noche.
Ehs deh NOH-cheh.

It's night, evening.

Es/ temprano/ tarde/.
Ehs /tehm-PRAH-noh/ TAHR-deh/.

It's/ early/ late/.

Se hace tarde.
Seh AH-seh TAHR-deh.

It's getting late.

Un rato.
Oon RAH-toh.

A short while.

Lo antes posible.
Loh AHN-tehs poh-SEE-bleh.

As soon as possible.

117

Vale más una imagen que mil palabras.

A picture is worth a thousand words.

CANTIDADES

QUANTITIES

¿Cuántos años tienes?
¿KWAHN-tohs AHN-yohs t'YEH-nehs?

How old are you?

¿Cuántos años tiene/ mami/ papi/?
¿KWAHN-tohs AHN-yohs t'YEH-neh/
MAH-mee/PAH-pee/?

How old is/ mommy/daddy/?

¿Cuántos dedos ves?
¿KWAHN-tohs DEH-dohs behs?

How many fingers do you see?

¿Cuántos hay?
¿KWAHN-tohs igh?

How many are there?

Hay solamente uno de ellos.
Igh soh-lah-MEHN-teh OO-noh deh EH-yohs.

There is only one of them.

Hay solamente cuatro de ellos.
Igh soh-lah-MEHN-teh KWAH-troh deh
EH-yohs

There are only four of them.

No tengo ninguno (de ellos).
Noh TEHN-goh neen-GOO-noh (deh EH-yohs).

I have none (of them).

118

No hay ninguno.
Noh igh neen-GOO-noh.

There are none.

Pon cada uno en su lugar.
Pohn KAH-dah OO-noh ehn soo loo-GAHR.

Put each one in its place.

Todas las galletitas han sido comidas.
TOH-dahs lahs gah-yeh-TEE-tahs ahn
SEE-doh koh-MEE-dahs.

All the cookies have been eaten.

No hay más galletitas.
Noh igh mahs gah-yeh-TEE-tahs.

There are no more cookies.

Después de quince viene dieciseis.
Dehs-PWEHS deh KEEN-seh b'YEH-neh
d'yehs-ee-SEH-eehs.

After fifteen comes sixteen.

Cuenta de tres a diez.
KWEHN-tah deh trehs ah d'YEHS.

Count from three to ten.

Uno más uno son dos.
OO-noh mahs OO-noh sohn dohs.

One and one make two.

Cuatro menos tres son uno.
KWAH-troh MEH-nohs trehs sohn OO-noh.

Four minus three make one.

Dos por uno son dos.
Dohs pohr OO-noh sohn dohs.

Two times one make two.

Seis dividido por dos son tres.
SEH-ees dee-bee-DEE-doh pohr dohs
sohn trehs.

Six divided by two make three.

Dos, cuatro, seis son números pares.
Dohs, KWAH-troh, SEH-ees sohn
NOO-meh-rohs PAH-rehs.

Two, four, six are even numbers.

Tres, cinco, siete son núimeros impares.
Trehs, SEEN-koh, s'YEH-teh sohn NOO-meh-
rohs eem-PAH-rehs.

Three, five, seven are odd numbers.

dos mitades
dohs mee-TAH-dehs

two halves

una mitad, un tercio, un cuarto
OO-nah mee-TAHD, oon TEHR-s'yoh, oon
KWAHR-toh

one half, one third,
one fourth

un poco/ más/ menos/
oon POH-koh/ mahs/ MEH-nohs/

a little/ more/ less/

algunos/as (or) unos/as
ahl-GOO-nohs/ nahs (or) OO-nohs/ nahs

some (m/f)

unos/as (or) pocos/as
OO-nohs/ ahs (or) POH-kohs/ kahs

a few (m/f)

muchos/as
MOO-chohs/ chahs

many, a lot, several (m/f)

bastante
bah-STAHN-teh

enough

cero	0	siete	7
SEH-roh		s'YEH-teh	
uno	1	ocho	8
OO-noh		OH-choh	
dos	2	nueve	9
dohs		NWEH-beh	
tres	3	diez	10
trehs		d'YEHS	
cuatro	4	once	11
KWAH-troh		OHN-seh	
cinco	5	doce	12
SEEN-koh		DOH-seh	
seis	6	trece	13
SEH-ees		TREH-seh	

catorce kah-TOHR-seh	14		cuarenta kwah-REHN-tah	40
quince KEEN-seh	15		cuarenta y uno kwah-REHN-tah ee OO-noh	41
dieciseis d'yehs-ee-SEH-ees	16		cincuenta seen-KWEHN-tah	50
diecisiete d'yehs-ee-s'YEH-teh	17		cincuenta y uno seen-KWEHN-tah ee OO-noh	51
dieciocho d'yehs-ee-OH-choh	18			
diecinueve d'yehs-ee-NWEH-beh	19		sesenta seh-SEHN-tah	60
veinte BAIN-teh	20		sesenta y uno seh-SEHN-tah ee OO-noh	61
veintiuno bain-tee-OO-noh	21		setenta seh-TEHN-tah	70
veintidos bain-tee-DOHS	22		setenta y uno seh-TEHN-tah ee OO-noh	71
veintitres bain-tee-TREHS	23		ochenta oh-CHEHN-tah	80
treinta TRAIN-tah	30		ochenta y uno oh-CHEHN-tah ee OO-noh	81
treinta y uno TRAIN-tah ee OO-noh	31		noventa noh-BEHN-tah	90
treinta y dos TRAIN-tah ee dohs	32		noventa y uno noh-BEHN-tah ee OO-noh	91
treinta y tres TRAIN-tah ee trehs	33			

ciento (cien)** 100
s'YEHN-toh (s'YEHN)

ciento uno 101
s'YEHN-toh OO-noh

ciento dos 102
s'YEHN-toh dohs

doscientos 200
dohs-s'YEHN-tohs

doscientos uno 201
dohs-s'YEHN-tohs
OO-noh

trescientos 300
trehs-s'YEHN-tohs

cuatrocientos 400
kwah-troh-s'YEHN-
tohs

quinientos 500
keen-YEHN-tohs

seiscientos 600
seh-ees-s'YEHN-tohs

setecientos 700
seh-teh-s'YEHN-tohs

ochocientos 800
oh-choh-s'YEHN-tohs

novecientos 900
noh-beh-s'YEHN-
tohs

mil 1000
meel

dos mil 2000
dohs meel

tres mil, quinientos
cinco 3,505
trehs meel, keen-YEHN-
tohs SEEN-koh

cien mil 100,000
s'YEHN meel

un millón (followed
by "de") 1,000,000
oon mee-YOHN (deh)

dos millones (followed
by "de") 2,000,000
dohs mee-YOHN-ehs
(deh)

**Note: Ciento becomes cien when standing alone or before nouns and before
the numbers mil and millones. In all other numbers, the full form of ciento is used.

Se aprenda con la práctica. Practice makes perfect.

ALFABETO   ALPHABET

A	B	C	CH	D	E	F	G
ah	beh	seh	cheh	deh	eh	EH-feh	ghey

H	I	J	(*K)	L	LL	M	N
AH-cheh	ee	HOH-tah		EH-leh	EH-yeh	EH-meh	EH-neh

Ñ	O	P	Q	R	RR	S	T
EH-nyeh	oh	peh	koo	EH-reh	EH-rreh	EH-seh	teh

U	V	(*W)	X	Y	Z
OO	beh		EH-kees	ee-gr'YEH-gah	SEH-tah

*K and W are not found in words of Spanish origin.

¿Qué letra es esta?   What letter is this?
¿Keh LEH-trah ehs EH-stah?

Aquí está la letra A.   Here is the letter A.
Ah-KEE ehs-TAH lah LEH-trah ah.

123

Lee esta letra.
LEH-yeh EHS-tah LEH-trah.

Read this letter.

¿Cuántas letras hay en la palabra gato?
¿KWAHN-tahs LEH-trahs igh ehn lah
pah-LAH-brah GAH-toh?

How many letters are there
in the word cat?

¿Dónde está la letra H?
¿DOHN-deh ehs-TAH lah LEH-trah
AH-cheh?

Where is the letter H?

Indica la letra J.
Een-DEE-kah lah LEH-trah HOH-tah.

Point to the letter J.

¿Qué quiere decir esta palabra?
¿Keh k'YEH-reh deh-SEER EHS-tah
pah-LAH-brah?
(or)
¿Qué significa esta palabra?
¿Keh seeg-nee-FEE-kah EHS-tah
pah-LAH-brah?

What does this word mean?

What does this word mean?

¿De quién es este nombre?
¿Deh k'YEHN ehs EHS-teh NOHM-breh?

Whose name is this?

No agarres el lápiz tan fuerte.
Noh ah-GAH-rrehs el LAH-pees tahn
FWEHR-teh.

Don't hold your pencil so tightly.

Agárralo así.
Ah-GAH-rrah-loh ah-SEE.

Hold it like this.

Escribe hacia abajo y después hacia la
derecha para la L.
Ehs-KREE-beh ah-SEE-ah ah-BAH-hoh
ee dehs-PWEHS ah-SEE-ah lah deh-
REH-chah PAH-rah lah EH-leh.

Write down and then to the
right for L.

124

Cada quien con su cada cual.   Birds of a feather flock together.

CANCIONES   INFANTILES   NURSERY   RHYMES

Nursery rhymes are a marvelous way to soothe a crying baby, fill a few empty
minutes, or just enjoy for their own rhythm. Hearing these rhymes will also give
the listener a feel for the rhythm of the language. Trusting that the reader already
knows the English version of these rhymes, we have chosen to translate them more
closely to the Spanish text so that, even though stilted at times, the literal translation
of the Spanish words will be understood by the reader. The feeling of the rhymes
are, for the most part, the same whether in Spanish or English.

TO MARKET, TO MARKET

LET'S GO TO THE FAIR
TO BUY A LITTLE PIG.
NOW WE BRING IT
HOME TO TAKE CARE OF IT.

LET'S GO TO THE FAIR
TO SELL A FAT HOG.
AGAIN HOME
TO EAT WELL!

RAIN, RAIN

RAIN, RAIN,
GET AWAY FROM HERE.
GO TO SCOTLAND.
DON'T GET ME WET.

A la Feria, A la Feria

Vamos a la feria
un cerdito a comprar.
Ahora lo llevamos
a casa a cuidar.

Vamos a la feria
un gran puerco a vender.
Otra vez a casa
para bien comer!

Lluvia, Lluvia

Lluvia, lluvia,
vete de aquí.
Vete a Escocia.
No me mojes a mí.

125

THE THREE LITTLE KITTENS

THE THREE LITTLE KITTENS,
LOST THEIR MITTENS
AND THEY BEGAN TO CRY.
MOTHER, MOTHER, WE HAVE TO CONFESS
THAT OUR MITTENS HAVE BEEN LOST.

WHAT NAUGHTY KITTENS,
TO LOSE YOUR MITTENS!
FOR THAT, YOU WILL HAVE NO PIE!
MEOW, MEOW, MEOW, MEOW.
THEN NO, YOU WILL HAVE NO PIE!

THE THREE LITTLE KITTENS
FOUND THEIR MITTENS
AND ANEW THEY BEGAN TO CRY.
MOTHER, MOTHER, WE CAN TELL YOU
THAT WE HAVE JUST FOUND THEM.

PUT ON YOUR LITTLE MITTENS,
SILLY KITTENS,
AND I WILL GIVE YOU A PIE.
PURR, PURR, PURR, PURR.
HOW RICH IS OUR PIE!

Los Tres Gatitos

Los tres gatitos
perdieron sus guantecitos
y se pusieron a llorar.
Mamá, mamá, tenemos que confesar
que los guantes se han perdido.

¡Qué malos gatitos,
perder los guantecitos!
¡Por eso, no tendréis pastel!
Miau, miau, miau, miau.
¡Pues no, no tendréis pastel!

Los tres gatitos
encontraron sus guantecitos
y de nuevo se pusieron a llorar.
Mamá, mamá, ya te podemos avisar
que los acabamos de encontrar.

Poneos los guantecitos,
majaderos gatitos,
y os daré un pastel.
Ronrón, ronrón, ronrón, ronrón.
¡Qué rico es nuestro pastel!

HUMPTY DUMPTY

HUMPTY DUMPTY SAT ON A WALL.
HUMPTY DUMPTY FELL VERY HARD.
NEITHER THE CIVIL GUARD NOR THE
CALVARY KNEW HOW HE WOULD
BE PUT TOGETHER.

Jamti Damti

Jamti Damti se sentó en un muro.
Jamti Damti se cayó muy duro.
Ni la Guardia Civil ni la Caballería
supieron como se incorporaría.

THREE BLIND MICE

SEE HOW THEY RUN,
THE THREE BLIND MICE!
HOW THEY RUN AND HOW THEY RUN
AFTER THE FARMER'S WIFE
WHO CUTS OFF THEIR TAILS
WITH A BUTCHER'S KNIFE.
HAVE YOU SEEN IN YOUR LIFE
SUCH SILLIES?
THE THREE BLIND MICE...!

Los Tres Ratones Ciegos

¡Mira cómo corren,
los tres ratones ciegos!
Que corren y que corren
tras la mujer del granjero
que les corta el rabo
con cuchillo de carnicero.
¿Has visto en tu vida
tales majaderos?
¡Los tres ratones ciegos, los tres ratones ciegos!

LITTLE BO-PEEP

THE FLOCK LEFT LITTLE BO-PEEP
AND SHE DOESN'T FIND THE TRAIL.
LEAVE THEM ALONE AND THEY'LL
COME BY THEMSELVES
CARRYING THEIR TAILS IN VIEW.

BO-PEEP, BEFORE LEAVING, FELL ASLEEP,
AND DREAMED SHE HEARD THEM BLEATING;
BUT WHEN SHE AWOKE,
SHE SAW IT WAS A TRICK
AND THAT HER SHEEP WERE WANDERING.

SHE GRABBED FIRMLY HER STICK
TO GO OUT TO SEARCH FOR THEM;
BUT WHEN SHE FOUND THEM,
SHE SWOONED
BECAUSE THEY HAD LOST THEIR TAILS.

IT HAPPENED ONE DAY,
WHEN BO-PEEP WAS WALKING,
IN A MEADOW NEARBY,
SHE FOUND THEIR TAILS IN A ROW,
HANGING TO DRY.

SHE SIGHED WITH RELIEF,
DRIED A LITTLE TEAR
AND DEPARTED FOR THE HILL HOPPING,
KNOWING IT WAS HER LITTLE DUTY
TO JOIN EACH TAIL WITH ITS LAMB.

La Pequeño Bo-Pip

A la pequeño Bo Pip se le fue el rebaño
y ya no enquentra la pista,
Dejadlos tranquilos, y vendrán solitos,

Llevando la cola a la vista.

Bo Pip, antes de salir, se puso a dormir,
y soño que los oía balando;
pero cuando se despertó,
vió que era un engaño
y que sus ovejas andaban vagando.

Cogió en firme su cayado
para salir a buscarlas;
pero cuando las encontró
se desmayó
porque, habían perdido la cola.

Sucedió que un día,
cuando Bo Pip andaba,
en un prado de ese lugar,
encontró las colas en fila,
tendidas a sacar.

Suspiró con alivio,
se secó una lagrimita
y salió por el monte dando salitos,
sabiendo que era su debercito
juntar cada cola con su corderito.

127

Padre Nuestro

Padre nuestro, que estás en el cielo,
santificado sea tu nombre;
venga tu reino,
hágase tu voluntad
en la tierra como en el cielo.
Danos hoy nuestro pan de cada día;
perdona nuestras ofensas como también
nosotros perdonamos a los que nos ofenden;
no nos dejes caer en tentación,
y líbranos del mal. Amén

Our Father

Our Father who art in heaven,
hallowed be thy name;
thy kingdom come,
thy will be done
on earth as it is in heaven.
Give us this day our daily bread;
forgive us our trespasses as also
we forgive those who offend us;
lead us not into temptation,
and deliver us from evil. Amen.

Salmo 23

El Señor es mi pastor;
nada me faltará.
En prados de tiernos pastos
me hace descansar.
Junto a aguas tranquilas me conduce.
Confortará mi alma
y me guiará por sendas de justicia
por amor de su nombre.

Aunque ande en valle de sombra de muerte,
no temeré mal alguno,
porque tú estarás conmigo
Tu vara y tu cayado me infundirán aliento.

Preparas mesa delante de mí
en presencia de mis adversarios.
Unges mi cabeza con aceite;
mi copa está rebosando.

Ciertamente el bien y la misericordia
me seguirán todos los días de mi vida,
y en la casa del Señor
moraré por días sin fin.

Psalm 23

The Lord is my shepherd;
there is nothing I shall want.
In verdant pastures
He gives me repose.
Beside restful waters He leads me;
He refreshes my soul.
He guides me in right paths
for his name's sake.

Though I walk in the dark valley
I will fear no evil;
for you are at my side.
Your rod and staff give me courage.

You prepare the table before me
in the sight of my foes;
You anoint my head with oil;
my cup overflows.

Only goodness and kindness
follow me all the days of my life;
And I shall dwell in the house
of the Lord for years to come.

Oración antes de Comer

Bendícenos, Señor, a nosotros y estos
donos tuyos que vamos a tomar y que
hemos recibido de tu generosidad. Amén.

Prayer before Meals

Bless us, O Lord, and these
your gifts which we are about to
receive from your goodness. Amen.

VOCABULARY

The Family and Other Persons

mami, mamá/ madre	mommy/mother
papi, papá/ padre	daddy/father
la abuela	grandmother
el abuelo	grandfather
la abuelita	grandma
el abuelito	grandpa
la tía	aunt
el tío	uncle
la prima	cousin (f)
el primo	cousin (m)
la sobrina	niece
el sobrino	nephew
la nieta	granddaughter
el nieto	grandson
la hija	daughter
el hijo	son
la hermana	sister
el hermano	brother
la mujer, la señora	woman
el hombre, el señor	man
la chica, la muchacha	girl
el chico, el muchacho	boy
los chicos, los muchachos	children
Señor	Mister
Señora	Missus
Señorita	Miss

Endearments

mi bebé	my baby
mi muñeca	my doll
mi princesa	my princess
mi principito	my little prince
mi tesoro	my treasure
cariño (a)	sweetheart
mi querido (a)	my dear
mi chiquito (a)	my little one
mi vida	my life
mi cielo	my sky
mi corazón	my heart

Colors

verde	green
azul	blue
negro (a)	black
blanco (a)	white
naranja	orange
rojo (a)	red
amarillo (a)	yellow
violeta	violet
rosa	pink
morado (a)	purple
café	brown (med)
marrón	brown (dark)
gris	gray
avano (a)	beige

Days of the Week

el lunes	Monday
el martes	Tuesday
el miércoles	Wednesday
el jueves	Thursday
el viernes	Friday
el sábado	Saturday
el domingo	Sunday

Months of the Year

enero	January
febrero	February
marzo	March
abril	April
mayo	May
junio	June
julio	July
agosto	August

130

septiembre	September		Nursery	
octubre	October		la bañera	bath tub
noviembre	November		el libro	book
diciembre	December		el coche del bebé	carriage
			el moisés	cradle
Seasons of the Year			la cuna	crib
			el pañal	diaper
el invierno	winter		la mamadera	feeding bottle
la primavera	spring		la silla alta	high chair
el verano	summer		Madre Oca	Mother Goose
el otoño	autumn		la lámpara de noche	night light
			el chupete	pacifier
			el pañal desechable	Pamper
Holidays of the Year			el cuadro	picture
			el corral	play pen
el cumpleaños	birthday		la mecedora	rocker
el cumpleaños de Jorge Washington	George Washington-ton's Birthday		el cochecito	stroller
el cumpleaños de Abraham Lincoln	Abraham Lincoln's Birthday		el juguete	toy
el día de San Valentín	St. Valentine's Day		**Toys**	
			la pelota	ball
el día de San Patricio	St. Patrick's Day		el globo	balloon
			el bate	bat
la Pascua (de los judios)	Passover		la bolita	bead
			la bicicleta	bicycle
la Pascua	Easter (season)		el cubo	block
la Semana Santa	Easter (Holy)Week		el bote (velero)	boat (sail)
la Pascua de Resurreción	Easter Sunday		el bull dozer	bull dozer
			el autobús	bus
el día de las madres	Mother's Day		el coche	car
el día de los padres	Father's Day		el tablero de ajedrez	chess board
el cuatro de julio	July 4th		la plasticina	clay
el doce de octubre	October 12th		el payaso	clown
la víspera de Todos los Santos	Halloween		el computador	computer
			el vaquero	cowboy
el día de acción de gracias	Thanksgiving Day		el crayón	crayon
			la muñeca	doll
la Navidad	Christmas		la casa de muñecas	doll house
la víspera del Año Nuevo	New Year's Eve		el tambor	drum
			el arete	earring
			la caña de pescar	fishing rod

131

el fuerte	fort	el submarino	submarine
el juego	game	el columpio	swing
el globo	globe	el tanque (militar)	tank (military)
el helicóptero	helicopter	el juego de té	tea service
el aro	hoop	el osito	teddy bear
la trompeta	horn	la raqueta de tenis	tennis racquet
el indio	Indian	la tienda de campaña	tent
el jeep	jeep	el trompo	top
el lazo de saltar	jump rope	la caja de juguetes	toy box
la cometa	kite	el tractor	tractor
la canica	marble	el tren (eléctrico)	train (electric)
la máscara	mask	el triciclo	tricycle
el collar	necklace	el camión	truck
la caja de pinturas	paint box	el volquete	dump truck
el pincel	paint brush	el camión de los	fire truck
el engrudo	paste	bomberos	
el libro de colorear	picture book	el camión de	garbage truck
la alcancía	piggy bank	basura	
el avión (a chorro)	plane (jet)	el camión de	oil truck
el maniquí	puppet	aceite	
el rompecabezas	puzzle	la grúa	tow truck
el coche de carreras	race car	el carretón	wagon
el rastrillo	rake	la carretilla	wheelbarrel
el sonajero	rattle	el pito	whistle
el anillo	ring	el xilófono	xylophone
el cohete	rocket ship		
el caballo mecedor	rocking horse	Clothing	
la cuerda	rope	la mochila	backpack
la caja de arena	sandbox	el traje de baño	bathing suit
las tijeras	scissors	la bata de baño	bathrobe
el patinete	scooter	el babero	bib
el sube y baja	see-saw	la blusa	blouse
la pala	shovel	la bota	boot
el patin	skate (ice)	la gorra	cap
el monopatín	skateboard	el abrigo	coat
el trineo	sled	el vestido	dress
el tobogán	slide	el guante	glove
el soldadito	soldier (lead)	el pañuelo	handkerchief
(de plomo)		el sombrero	hat
el soldadito	soldier (wooden)	el zapato de	high heel (pump)
(de madera)		tacón alto	

la chaqueta	jacket	el ombligo	belly button
el blue jean	jeans	la mejilla	cheek
el mitón	mitten	el pecho	chest
la bata de dormir	nightgown	la barbilla	chin
el overol	overalls	la oreja	ear
el abrigo	overcoat	el codo	elbow
las pijamas	pajamas	el ojo	eye
la cartera	pocketbook	la ceja	eyebrow
el impermeable	raincoat	el párpado	eyelid
la bota de goma	rubber boot	los ojos	eyes
la sandalia	sandal	la cara	face
la bufanda	scarf	el dedo	finger
la camisa	shirt	la uña	fingernail
el zapato	shoe	el pie	foot
el cordón (de zapato)	shoelace	la frente	forehead
los pantalones cortos	shorts	el pelo, el cabello	hair
la falda	skirt	la mano	hand
los pantalones	slacks	la cabeza	head
las enaguas	slip	el talón	heel
la zapatilla	slipper	la cadera	hip
el zapato de tenis	sneaker	la quijada	jaw
el traje de nieve	snow suit	la rodilla	knee
el calcetín	sock	la pierna	leg
la media	stocking	el labio	lip
el suéter	sweater	la boca	mouth
la camiseta	tee-shirt	el cuello	neck
la corbata	tie	la nariz	nose
las medias	tights	el hombro	shoulder
el paraguas	umbrella	el estómago	stomach
el cazoncillo	underpants	la garganta	throat
la camiseta	undershirt	el pulgar	thumb
la ropa interior	underwear	el dedo (del pie)	toe
la carterita	wallet	la lengua	tongue
la cremallera (or)	zipper	el diente	tooth
el cierre		la panza	tummy
		la cintura	waist
The Human Body		la muñeca	wrist
el tobillo	ankle		
el brazo	arm	**Beverages**	
la espalda	back		
el trasero	backside	la cerveza	beer
la panza	belly	Coca-Cola	Coca-Cola

133

		la remolacha	beet
el chocolate	cocoa (hot)	el brócoli	broccoli
(caliente)		el bretón	Brussel sprout
café (con leche)	coffee (with milk)	el repollo	cabbage
la gaseosa de limón	lemon soda	la zanahoria	carrot
la limonada	lemonade	el coliflor	cauliflower
la leche	milk	el apio	celery
el jugo de naranja	orange juice	el maíz	corn
la naranjada	orangeade	el choclo	(ear of) corn
la soda	soda (club soda)	el pepino	cucumber
el refresco (de uva,	soda (grape, orange)	la berenjena	eggplant
de naranja)		el ajo	garlic
el té (una taza de)	tea (cup of)	la lechuga	lettuce
el té (con limón)	tea (with lemon)	el champiñon, hongo	mushroom
el agua (con hielo)	water (with ice)	la cebolla	onion
el vino	wine	el perejil	parsley
el vino tinto	red wine	el guisante, la arveja	pea
el vino blanco	white wine	el pimentón	pepper
		la papa	potato

Desserts

		la calabaza	pumpkin
la tarta de manzana	apple pie	el rábano	radish
la torta	cake	el alga marina	seaweed
el dulce	candy	la espinaca	spinach
la galletita	cookie	el zapallo	squash
el flan	custard	la judia verde	stringbean
el flan de caramelo	caramel custard	el tornate	tomato
el flan de	chocolate	el nabo	turnip
chocolate	custard		
el flan de vainilla	vanilla custard		

Meat

la gelatina	gelatin	el tocino	bacon
el (cono de) helado	ice cream (cone)	el pollo (asado)	chicken (roasted)
el panqueque	pancake	el perrito caliente	frankfurter/
el pastel de ...	pastry		hot dog
la torta	pound cake	el jamón	ham
de mantequilla		la hamburguesa	hamburger
el budín	pudding	la chuleta de cordero	lamb chop
el budín de arroz	rice pudding	la pata del cordero	leg of lamb
el yogurt	yoghurt	la chuleta de cerdo	pork chop
		la salchicha	sausage

Vegetables

| | | el bistek | steak |
| el espárrago | asparagus | el pavo | turkey |

134

Seafood

la carpa	carp
el bacalao	cod
el pejerrey	flounder
el arenque	herring
la langosta	lobster
el salmón	salmon
la sardina	sardine
el camarón	shrimp
el lenguado	sole
la trucha	trout
el atún	tuna

Fruits

la manzana	apple
la salsa de manzana	applesauce
el albaricoque	apricot
el plátano	banana
el mirtilo	blueberry
la cereza	cherry
el coco	coconut
la uva	grape
la toronja	grapefruit
las uvas (racimo de)	grapes (bunch)
el limón	lemon
la naranja	orange
el durazno	peach
la pera	pear
la piña	pineapple
la ciruela	plum
la ciruela seca	prune
la pasa (de uva)	raisin
la frambuesa	raspberry
la fresa	strawberry
la mandarina	tangerine
la sandía	watermelon

Other Foods

el pan	bread
el pancillo	bun
la mantequilla	butter
el cereal	cereal
el queso	cheese
la goma de mascar	chewing-gum
el algodón de azúcar	cotton candy
la galleta	cracker
la crema	cream
la miga	crumb
el huevo	egg
el huevo frito	fried egg
el huevo duro	hard-boiled egg
los huevos revueltos	scrambled eggs
las papas fritas	French fries
la salsa	gravy
la miel	honey
las conservas	jam
la mermelada	jelly
la salsa de tomate	ketchup
el puré de papas	mashed potatoes
el chocolate	milk chocolate
la mostaza	mustard
los fideos	noodle
la avena	oatmeal
el panqueque	pancake
el maní	peanut
la mantequilla de maní	peanut butter
la pimienta	pepper
el encurtido	pickle
las palomitas de maíz	popcorn
las papas fritas	potato chips
el arroz	rice
el pancillo	roll
la ensalada	salad
la sal	salt
el emparedado	sandwich
la salsa	sauce
el chocrut	sauerkraut
la sopa (de legumbres)	soup (vegetables)
los espaguetis	spaghetti
el cocido	stew

135

el almíbar	syrup	la jarra	jar
la tostada	toast	la tapa	top,cover
el vinagre	vinegar	el tubo	tube
		el envoltorio	wrapper

Tableware

la botella	bottle	House	
el plato hondo	bowl	el desván	attic
la cremera	creamer	la puerta trasera	back door
la taza	cup	el jardín	back yard
el plato de postre	dessert plate	el sótano	basement
el tenedor	fork	el baño	bathroom
el vaso	glass	el dormitorio	bedroom
la tetera	kettle	el techo	ceiling
el cuchillo	knife	la chimenea	chimney
la servilleta	napkin	el comedor	dining room
el sartén	pan	el salón de estar	family room/den
la jarra	pitcher	la cerca	fence
el plato	plate	el piso	floor
la fuente	platter	la puerta principal	front door
la olla	pot	el jardín	garden
la olla pequeña	saucepan	la puerta	gate
el platito	saucer	el pasillo	hallway
el sartén	skillet	la cocina	kitchen
el sopero	soup plate	el pasto	lawn
la cuchara	spoon	la regadera	lawn sprinkler
la azucarera	sugar bowl	la sala	living room
el mantel	tablecloth	el buzón	mail box
la cuchara	tablespoon	el techo	roof
la tetera	teapot	la escalera	stair
la cucharita	teaspoon	el escalón	step
la bandeja	tray	la pared	wall
		la ventana	window
		el patio	yard

Containers

el saco, la bolsa	bag	Dwellings	
la botella	bottle	el apartamento	apartment
la caja	box	el búngalo	bungalow
la lata	can	la cabina	cabin
la caja de cartón	carton	el condominio	condominium
la jaula	crate	la casa de campo	country house
el sobre	envelope		

el hotel	hotel	el tostador	toaster
la tienda de campaña	tent	la máquina de	typewriter
la casa rodante	trailer,	escribir	
	mobile home	la aspiradora	vacuum cleaner
		la cera (para muebles)	wax (furniture)

Kitchen

el delantal	apron	**Bedroom**	
la escoba	broom	la butaca	armchair
el gabinete de	broom closet	la cama	bed
las escobas		la cubrecama	bedspread
el gabinete	cabinet	la manta	blanket
el reloj	clock	la persiana	blind (Venetian)
la secadora	clothes dryer	la alfombra	carpet
la lavaropa	clothes washer	la silla	chair
el mostrador	counter	la colgador	coat hanger
la alacena	cupboard	la cortina	curtain
el detergente	detergent	la cómoda	dresser
el trapo	dish cloth	la lámpara	lamp
el lavaplatos	dish washer	el colchón	mattress
el trapo	dust cloth	el espejo	mirror
el recogedor de	dust pan	el tocadiscos	phonograph
basura		la almohada	pillow
el plomero	duster	el enchufe	plug/electric
el batidor de huevo	egg beater		outlet
el batidor eléctrico	electric beater	la colcha	quilt
el embudo	funnel	la mecedora	rocking chair
la plancha	iron	el visillo	shade
la tabla de planchar	ironing board	la sábana	sheet
el (horno de)	microwave	la persiana	shutter
microondas	(oven)	el estereo	stereo
el trapeador	mop	el velador	table (night)
el balde	pail		
la olla (grande)	pot (large)	**Living Room**	
la nevera, heladera	refrigerator	el aire acondicionado	air-conditioner
la máquina de coser	sewing machine	el estante	book shelf
el fregadero	sink	el estante	bookcase
la esponja	sponge	el sofá	couch
el taburete	stool	la chimenea	fireplace
la estufa	stove	el piano	piano
el colador	strainer	el cuadro	picture
la mesa	table	la radio (de onda	radio set
		corta)	(short wave)

la grabadora	recorder (cassette)	el restaurante	restaurant
el teléfono	telephone	el fútbol	soccer
el televisor	television set	los deportes	sports
la video-	VCR	la natación	swimming
grabadora		el zoológico (or)	zoo
		el zoo	

Bathroom

la aspirina	aspirin		
la toalla	bath towel	**Tools**	
la bañera	bathtub	la hacha	axe
la colonia	cologne	la escoba	broom
la toallita de la cara	face cloth	el martillo	hammer
la crema de la cara	face cream	la manguera	hose
el lápiz de labio	lipstick	la escalera	ladder
el esmalte	nail polish	el cortacésped	lawn mower
el perfume	perfume	el clavo	nail
el talco	powder	la tuerca	nut
la hoja de afeitar	razor blade	el zapapico	pick
la máquina de afeitar	razor (electric)	la horca	pitch fork
el jabón de afeitar	shaving soap	los alicates	pliers
el lavamanos	sink	el rastrillo	rake
el jabón	soap	el papel de lijar	sandpaper
el inodoro	toilet bowl	el serrucho	saw
el papel higénico	toilet paper	las tijeras	scissors
el cepillo de dientes	toothbrush	el tornillo	screw
la pasta de dientes	toothpaste	el destornillador	screwdriver
		la pala	shovel

Entertainments

		la espada	spade
el acuario	aquarium	la llama	trowel
el béisbol	baseball	el tornillo de banco	vise
el baloncesto	basketball	la carretilla	wheelbarrow
el juego de boleo	bowling	la llave inglesia	wrench (adjustable)
el circo	circus		
el concierto	concert		
el fútbol americano	football	**Along the Road**	
el partido	game, match	el aeropuerto	airport
el cine	movie	la panne	breakdown
el cínema	movie theatre	el puente	bridge
el museo	museum	el ómnibus	bus (school)
el recreo	recess (at school)	(del colegio)	

el edificio	building	el auto deportivo	sports car
el edificio de	apartment	la calle	street
apartamentos	building	el farol	street light
el edificio de	office building	el taxi	taxi
oficinas		la casilla del	telephone booth
la estación	bus station	teléfono	
de autobús		el poste del teléfono	telephone pole
la parada	bus stop	el riel	track (railroad)
de autobús		el tráfico	traffic
el coche	car	el circulo de tráfico	traffic circle
el lavadero de coches	car-wash	la congestión de	traffic jam
la iglesia	church	tráfico	
la esquina	corner	el semáforo	traffic light
el andén	curb	el tren	train
el autopista	expressway	la estación de tren	train station
la fábrica	factory	el camión	truck
la cerca	fence	la camioneta	pick-up truck
el campo	field	la grúa	tow truck
la casa de los	fire house	el tunel	tunnel
bomberos		el van	van
la boca de agua	fire plug		
para incendios		The Car	
la rueda reventada	flat tire	el acelerador	accelerator
el seto	hedge	la antena	antenna
la carretera	highway	los frenos	brakes
hacer dedo	to hitch-hike	el parachoques	bumper
la casa	house	el tablero de	dashboard
la vía	lane	instrumentos	
el buzón	mail box	la puerta	door
la motocicleta	moped	la manecilla	door handle
la motocicleta	motorbike	el motor	engine
la moto	motorcycle	la guantera	glove compartment
la patineta	motorscooter	el faro	headlight
aparcar	to park	el capó	hood
el peatón	pedestrian	la bocina	horn
la oficina de correos	post office	la ignición	ignition
el camino	road	el gato	jack
la acera	sidewalk	la matrícula	license plate
la señal	sign post	la cerradura	lock
el carro de nieve	snow mobile	el retrovisor	mirror (of car)
el limite de velocidad	speed limit	la ventana trasera	rear window

el asiento	seat	el chófer de autobús	bus driver
el arranque	starter	el (la) carnicero (a)	butcher
automático		el (la) carpintero (a)	carpenter
el volante	steering wheel	el chófer	chauffeur
el visor	sunvisor	la criada que hace	cleaning woman
la llanta	tire	la limpieza	
el maletero	trunk	el (la) técnico(a)	computer
la rueda	wheel	de computador	technician
el parabrisas	windshield	el (la) cocinero(a)	cook
el limpiaparabrisas	windshield wiper	el (la) dentista	dentist
		el (la) doctor(a)	doctor

Stores

		el (la) ingeniero(a)	engineer
la panadería	bakery	el (la) granjero(a)	farmer
el banco	bank	el bombero	fireman
la peluquería	barber shop	el mecánico	mechanic
la peluquería	beauty shop	el (la) basurero(a)	garbage man
la carnicería	butcher shop	el (la) jardinero(a)	gardener
la lavandería	cleaners	el (la) tendero(a)	grocer
la tienda de ropa	clothing store	el (la) peluquero(a)	hairdresser
la lechería	dairy store	el (la) vendedor(a)	hardware store
el almacén	department store	de la ferretería	sales(wo)man
la farmacia	drug store	la ama de casa	housewife
la floristería	florist (shop)	el joyero	jeweler
la mueblería	furniture store	el (la) abogado(a)	lawyer
la estación de	gas station	el (la) biblio-	librarian
gasolina		tecario(a)	
el mercado	grocery store	la criada	maid
la ferretería	hardware store	el cartero	mailman
la joyería	jewelry store	el (la) comerciante	merchant
la lavandería	laundromat	el (la) ministro	minister
el depósito de	lumber yard	el (la) modelo	model
madera		el (la) enfermero (a)	nurse
el mercado	market	el (la) pintor (a)	painter
el vivero	nursery	el (la) farma-	pharmacist
la zapatería	shoe store	ceútico(a)	
		el piloto	pilot

Occupations

		el (la) policía	policeman
			(woman)
el (la) astronauta	astronaut	el sacerdote,	priest
el (la) niñerola	baby sitter	el cura	
el (la) panadero (a)	baker	el rabino	rabbi

140

el corredor	race car driver	el elefante	elephant
automovilista		el cervato	fawn
el marinero	sailor	el zorro	fox
el (la) vendedor (a)	salesman	el caniche	French poodle
	(saleswoman)	la rana	frog
la secretaria	secretary	la jirafa	giraffe
el serviente,	servant	la cabra	goat
el (la) criado (a)		el gorila	gorilla
el (la) vendedor (a)	shoe store sales-	el cornejillo de Indias	guinea pig
de zapatos	man	el hipopótamo	hippotamus
	(saleswoman)	el caballo	horse
el (la) dueño (a)	shop owner	el cordero	lamb
de la tienda		el leopardo	leopard
la azafata	stewardess	el león	lion
el sastre	tailor	la llama	llama
el chófer	taxi driver	el topo	mole
el (la) maestro (a)	teacher	el mono	monkey
el (la) profesor (a)		el ratón	mouse
el (la) ingeniero (a)	train engineer	el buey	ox
(de trenes)		el cerdo	pig
el (la) camionero (a)	truck driver	el cerdito	piglet
el (la) mecanó-	typist	el caballito	pony
grafo (a)		el perrito	puppy
el acomodador	usher	el cornejo	rabbit
la acomodadora	usherette	el mapache	raccoon
el camarero	waiter	la rata	rat
la camarera	waitress	el reno	reindeer
el vigilante del	zoo keeper	la foca	seal
zoológico		la oveja	sheep
		la culebra	snake

Animals		la ardilla	squirrel
el oso	bear	el tigre	tiger
el pájaro	bird	la tortuga	turtle
el toro	bull	la ballena	whale
el camello	camel	el lobo	wolf
el gato	cat	el gusano	worm (earth)
la vaca	cow	la cebra	zebra
el cocodrilo	crocodile		
el ciervo	deer	Birds	
el perro	dog	el mirlo	blackbird
el burro	donkey	el azulejo	bluebird

el canario	canary	la cigarra	cicada
el cardinal	cardinal	la cucaracha	cockroach
el pollito	chick	el grillo	cricket
el pollo	chicken	la libélula	dragonfly
el cuervo	crow	la pulga	flea
la paloma	dove	la mosca	fly
el pato	duck	el mosquito	gnat
el patito	duckling	el saltamontes	grasshopper
el águila	eagle	la abeja (de miel)	honey bee
el ganso	goose	la mariquita	lady bug
el gansarón	gosling	el mosquito	mosquito
el pájaro mosca	hummingbird	la polilla	moth
la alondra	lark	el cortón	praying mantis
el ruiseñor	nightingale	(la araña)	(spider)(not an insect)
el avestruz	ostrich	la avispa	wasp
la lechuza	owl		
el perico	parakeet	Trees	
el loro	parrot	el manzano	apple
el pavón	peacock	el abedul	birch
el pelicano	pelican	el cerezo	cherry
el pingüino	penguin	el árbol frutal	fruit tree
el faisán	pheasant	el abeto	hemlock
la paloma	pigeon	el arce	maple
el cuervo	raven	la encina	oak
el pechicolorado	robin	la palmera	palm
el gallo	rooster	el peral	pear
la gaviota	seagull	el pino	pine
el gorrión	sparrow	el ciruelo	plum
la cigueña	stork	el álamo	poplar
la golondrina	swallow	la sequoia	sequoia
el cisne	swan	la picea	spruce
el pavo	turkey	el sauce	willow
el pájaro carpintero	woodpecker		

Insects

la hormiga	ant
la aveja	bee
el abejarrón	bumblebee
la mariposa	butterfly
la oruga	caterpillar

Flowers

la azalea	azalea
el botón de oro	buttercup
el clavel	carnation
el crisántemo	chrysanthemum
la prímula	cowslip
el azafrán	crocus

142

el narciso	daffodil	la orquídea	orchid
la dalia	dahlia	el pensamiento	pansy
la margarita	daisy	la peonía	peony
el diente de león	dandelion	la petunia	petunia
la gardenia	gardenia	la estrella federal	poinsettia
el geranio	geranium	el rododendro	rhododendron
la flor de lis	iris	la rosa	rose
la lila	lilac	el girasol	sunflower
la azucena	lily	la arveja olorosa	sweet pea
el lirio de los valles	lily of the valley	el tulipán	tulip
la mimosa	mimosa	la violeta	violet

PRONUNCIATION GUIDE

The following information on pronunciation is provided to answer basic questions which may arise regarding correct Spanish pronunciation. Pronunciation for Spanish spoken in Spain and in Spanish America has been included in this guide.

VOWELS

All vowels in Spanish are short, pure sounds. For the most part, each vowel has only one basic sound. There are slight variations according to placement within the phrase or word.

A: is always pronounced like *a* in *cha-cha*. For example: cara (KAH-rah).

E: The usual sound of Spanish *e* is halfway between the *e* in *get* and the *a* in *gate*. For example: mesa (MEH-sah).

I: is always pronounced like the sound of *ee* in *see*. For example: sí (see).

O: is pronounced like the *o* in *soldier*. For example: pelota (peh-LOH-tah).

U: is pronounced like *oo* in *boot*. For example: usted (oos-TEHD).

Y: is a vowel when standing alone or when located at the end of a word. As such it is pronounced like *ee* in *see* . For example: y (ee).

CONSONANTS

B: as in English

C: is pronounced like the Spanish *z*. In Spanish America this means the sound of *s* as in *sing* . For example: cinco (SEEN-koh). In most of Spain this means the sound of *th* as in *thing*. For example: cinco (THEEN-koh). In all other cases *c* is hard like *c* in *carry* . For example: comer (koh-MEHR).

D: is generally pronounced as the English *d* in *dainty* i.e., softly. For example: dónde (DOHN-deh).

F: as in English

G: before an *e* or *i* is pronounced like the Spanish *j* i.e., like the *ch* sound in the Scottish word *loch*. For example: coger (koh-HEHR). In all other cases, g is pronounced hard as in *go*. For example: gato (GAH-toh).

H: always silent

J: Spanish *j* does not have an equivalent sound in English. It is formed in the throat, and is similar to the *ch* sound in the Scottish word *loch*. For example: bajo (BAH-hoh).

K: as in English

L: as in English

LL: is pronounced as one consonant in Spanish. In Spanish America it sounds like *y* in the word *year*. For example: lleno (YEH-noh). In Spain it is pronounced like *lli* in *million*. For example: lleno (LYEH-noh).

M: as in English

N: as in English

Ñ: is like the sound of *ni* in *onion*. For example: niño (NEE-nyoh).

P: as in English

Qu: in Spanish is pronounced like k and appears only before an *e* or an *i*. For example: quiero (kee-YEH-roh).

R: is pronounced like a strong trill. For example: para (PAH-rah).

RR: is very strongly trilled. For example: perro (PEH-rroh).

S: is pronounced like the *s* in *see*. For example: casa (KAH-sah).

T: as in English.

V: like the *b* in *bad* only more softly. For example: vaso (BAH-soh).

X: before a consonant is pronounced as an English *s*. For example: explicar (ehs plee-KAHR). Between vowels, *x* is similar to the English *egz* in the word *exact*. For example: éxito (eks-ee-TOH).

Z: In Spanish America *z* is pronounced like the sound of *s* in the word *sing*. For example: zapato (sah-PAH-toh). In Spain *z* is pronounced like the sound *th* as in the word *think*. For example: zapato (thah-PAH-toh).

Linking is very important for accurate intonation. Briefly stated, the final vowel of a word must be joined with the beginning vowel of the following word (unless the words are separated by a comma or a pause). Tu abuelita; mi hermano.

A *diphthong* is a combination of any two vowels. Spanish vowels do not change their sound when forming a diphthong. They are pronounced more quickly in succession and form one syllable.

There is only one *accent mark* in Spanish: It is found over a vowel to indicate unexpected stress on that syllable. For example: automóvil. It is used with all interrogative words, and it differentiates two words which otherwise are spelled the same. For example: si - if; sí - yes. The accent mark does not affect the pronunciation of the vowel above which it is placed.

In words ending in a consonant, the last syllable is stressed. For example: pantalon (pahn-tah-LOHN). In words ending in a vowel, the next to the last syllable is stressed. For example: ahora (ah-OHR-rah).

For the purpose of this book, the Spanish pronunciation as spoken in Spanish America is used.

INDEX

A

to abandon	abandonar 80
(to be) able	poder 49
to add	agregar 54
All aboard!	¡Aborde! 80,89
(to be) afraid	tener miedo 35,47
after	después de 55
again	otra vez 39
air	el aire 86
airplane	el avión 57
(to be) all right	(estar) bien 40
alphabet	el alfabeto 123
all day	todo el día 24
all gone	eso es todo 28
allowance	la mesada 57
angry	enojado/a 104
animal	el animal 74
another	otro/a 34,35
answer	la repuesta 48
apple	la manzana 25
appointment	la cita 91
arm	el brazo 21,31,111
around	alrededor de 84,87
to arrive	llegar 89
to ask	preguntar 39,44
to ask a question	hacer pregunta 59
asleep	dormido/a 110
attic	el desván 93
awake	despierto/a 110

B

baby	el/ la/ bebé 35,45,53
back	la espalda, 18,95
back yard (grassy)	jardín trasero 76,93
backwards	hacia atrás 80,88,89
bacon	el tocino 24
bad	malo/a 108
to bake	cocer en horno 54
to bake	hacer 53,54,61
bakery	la panadería 69
baking powder	la levadura 54
balance	el equilibrio 78
ball	la pelota 33,77,88
balloon	el globo 86
banana	el plátano 25
bandaid	la curita 111
bargain	la ganga 67
to bark	ladrar 75
bat	el bate 77
bath	el baño 15,17
bathroom	el baño 16,19,48
bathtub	la bañera 18
battery	la batería 75
beach	la playa 93,105
to beat	revolver 54
beautiful	lindo/a 34,64
because	porque 44

D

daddy	papi 21,32,36
to dance	bailar 64
dangerous	peligroso/a 56
dark	la oscuridad 49
date	la fecha 58
day	el día 15
delicious	rico/a 28
to deliver	repartir 89
deodorant	el deodorante 18
to deserve	merecer (se) 63
to design	diseñar 84
dessert	el postre 26
diaper	el pañal 20
difficult	difícil 86
to dig	cavar 55,56
dinner	la cena 24,53
dirt	la tierra 76
dirty	sucio/a 16,41
dish	el plato 44,52
to disobey	desobedecer 40
to divide	dividir 106, 119
diving board	el trampolín 76
dizzy	mareado/a 111
to do/ make	hacer 40,43,45
to dock	entrar en el muelle 81
doctor	el médico 35
dog	el perro 37,51
doll	la muñeca 37,83
dollar	el dólar 68
done	hecho/a 54,66
door	la puerta 41
dough	la masa 54
downstairs	abajo 49
to drag	arrastrar 84
to draw	dibujar 64,82
to dream	soñar 30
dress	el vestido 80
to dress (oneself)	vestir (se) 83
dresser	la cómoda 22
to drink	tomar 26
to drive (into)	entrar en 89
to drive	manejar 76

driveway	el camino de entrada 88
to drop	dejar caer 43
drum	el tambor 34
to dry (dishes)	secar 52
to dry (oneself)	secar (se) 18
dull	desafilado/a 87
dust	el polvo 53
to dust	sacudir 53
dust cloth	el paño 53
to dye	teñir (se) 92

E

e-mail	correo electrónico 60
ear	la oreja 17,31
early	temprano 109
to eat	comer 21,23,25,26,27, 28,38,42
egg	el huevo 54
elbow	el codo 24
elevator	el ascensor 68
to empty	vaciar 19
enough	bastante 85
erase	borrar 83
error	el error 83
escalator	la escalera mecánica 68
everything	todo, 28,47,48
to excuse	perdonar 14
expensive	caro/a 68
extraordinary	extraordinario/a 101
eye	el ojo 31,65,81

F

face	la cara 16,17,27,47
(to make) faces	hacer caras 41
face cloth	la toallita de la cara 19
fair	limpio/a 80
fair	la feria 90
to fall	caer 41,85
family	la familia 19

G

H

I

J

K

to keep	mantener 77
to keep an eye	vigilar 96
to keep going	seguir 66,78
keyboard	el teclado 62
to kick	patear 33,37
kiss	el beso 14,110
kitchen	la cocina 42
kite	la cometa 85
knee	la rodilla 18
knife	el cuchillo 25,43
to knock	golpear 44
knot	el nudo 22
to know	conosco 31

L

lake	el lago 82, 93
to land	aterrizar 74
language	el vocabulario 45
lap	el regazo 30
large	grande 31
late	tarde 50
later	más tarde 19,39,40
to laugh	reir (se) 104
to launder	lavar 57
laundering	lavado/a 108
laundry	la ropa 54
lawn	el pasto 55
to lay	acostar (se) 83
leaf	la hoja 56
to leak	salir (se) 86
to lean	apoyar (se) 41
to leave	salir 77
to leave behind	dejar 27,63
to leave off	quedar 58
leg	la pierna 31,81
lesson	la lección 51
to let, leave	dejar 22,26,40
Let go!	¡Deja! 30,32,36
Let's go!	¡Vamonos! 49

letter	la letra 123,124
library	la biblioteca 50
license	el permiso 89
to lie down	acostar (se) 45
life	la vida 102
life boat	la lancha salvavida 80
to lift	levantar 87
light	la luz 43,49,109
like	como 31
to like	gustar 26,27,32,35
like this	así 124
line	la cola 69
to line up	hacer cola 85
to listen	escuchar 30,46,92
lit	prendido/a 109
little	poco 26
to load	carga 89
to look at	mirar 34,43
to look for	buscar 21
Look out!	¡Cuidado! 97
loose	suelto/a 97
to lose	perder 80
loud	fuerte 34
love	el amor 15
to lower	dejar caer 39
to lower	bajar 49,80
to be lucky	tener suerte 101
lunch	el almuerzo 21,43,95
(to have) lunch	almorzar 23

M

magazine	la revista 82
to make, do	hacer 38,45,53
to make a bed	hacer cama 52,53
make-up	el maquillaje 18
map	la mapa 59
marble (toy)	la canica 86
market	el mercado 67
to massage	darse masaje 32
match	el fósforo 43

S

T

WXYZ

COLOR, CUT and PASTE

A colorful, fun and easy way to get acquainted with this book is to match the pictures with the sentences in the text. The page number on the back of each drawing is given to help you spot the page you are looking for. An asterisk next to the appropriate sentence is also given to help you pinpoint the exact sentence. Sometimes a picture will match more than one sentence.

Spanish Bingo–

These pages can be used to play Bingo reenforcing learned Spanish vocabulary and of course, just for fun.

Look on pages 13 - 28 and match
these pictures with the correct sentences.

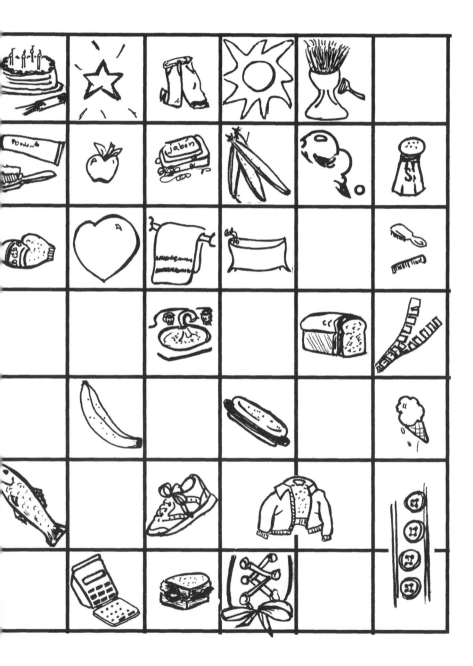

19   15   20   15   15

25   18   27   18   25   17

19   18   19   14   21

21   27   22

26   26   25

        21   20   26

21

        22   24   13

Look on pages 29 - 49 and match
these pictures with the correct sentences.

33   37   43   34

42   30   33

40   34   36

36   37   32   43

48   33   41

41   37   49

32   43   37   49

Look on pages 50 - 77 and match
these pictures with the correct sentences.

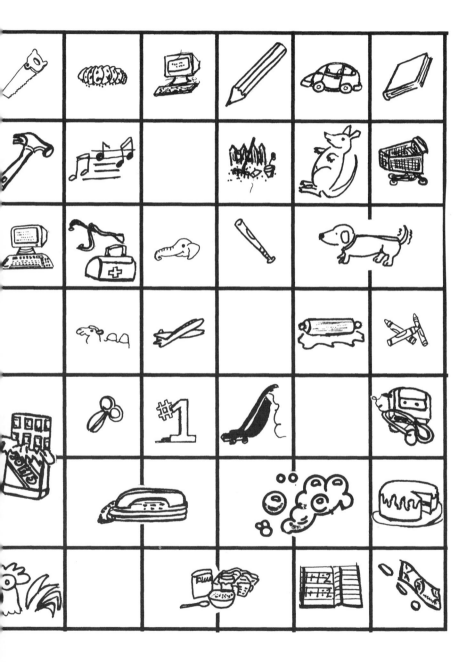

50   75   63   50   56   56

71   75   61   63
                                          56

    75   77   74   73   62

63   54   74   74

51   53   65   59

                                        63

53   76   66

68   60   54   75

Look on pages 78 - 114 and match
these pictures with the correct sentences.

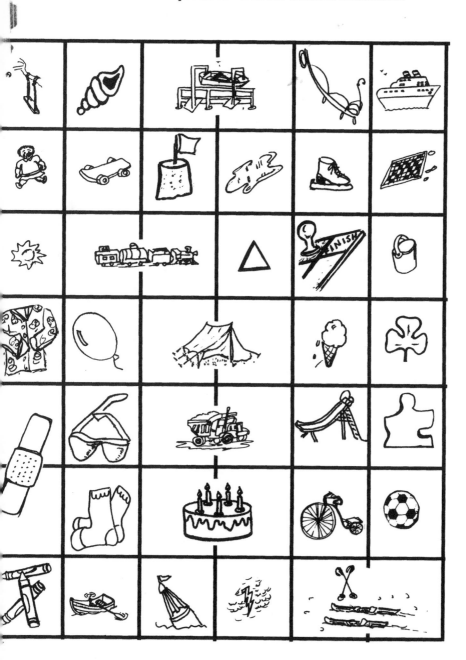

80   92   80   94   85

79   87   113   95   92   83

94   79   82   91   82

101   106   81   86   108

86   85   89   96   111

88   78   106   108

        96   114   95   81   83